Paschal Beverly Randolph

Seership! the Magnetic Mirror

A Practical Guide for Those Who Aspire to Clairvoyance-absolute

Paschal Beverly Randolph

Seership! the Magnetic Mirror
A Practical Guide for Those Who Aspire to Clairvoyance-absolute

ISBN/EAN: 9783744784306

Printed in Europe, USA, Canada, Australia, Japan

Cover: Foto ©ninafisch / pixelio.de

More available books at **www.hansebooks.com**

SEERSHIP!

THE MAGNETIC MIRROR.

A PRACTICAL GUIDE TO THOSE WHO ASPIRE TO

CLAIRVOYANCE-ABSOLUTE.

ORIGINAL AND SELECTED FROM VARIOUS EUROPEAN AND
ASIATIC ADEPTS.

BY

PASCHAL BEVERLY RANDOLPH.

BOSTON:

RANDOLPH AND COMPANY.

1870.

[NOTICE. — *There being but a* LIMITED *demand for a work of this character, only a* VERY SMALL EDITION *has been printed, and the cost thereof has
been divided among its purchasers equitably. If the work should ever be
enlarged and reprinted, it will be circulated at a price barely covering cost of
printing, binding, and advertising, as in the present case.*]

THE INNER SENSES.

I TRUST I may be pardoned if I make another attempt to rescue
the subject of somnambulic vision from the charlatanry of the day.
In these days clairvoyance, which is a natural power inherent in
the race, is regarded as a sort of forbidden, or rare, wonder, mixed
up with mesmerism, fraud, circles, and so on, while it is also the
garb under which more barefaced swindling is carried on than any
other one gift of God to civilized man. I hold it to be emphatically
true, that

> No curtain hides from view the spheres elysian,
>   Save these poor shells of half transparent dust;
> While all that blinds the spiritual vision
>   Is pride and hate and lust.

And I believe clairvoyance to be the birthright of every human
being; that *all* will one day possess it; that children will be born
so; and that even now, coarse as we are, some of us — a great percentage of the people — can develop it to a most surprising extent.
In the first place let it be distinctly understood that there are two
sources of light — solar, planetary, and astral — adapted to material eyes, and that, independent of that, every globe in space is
cushioned upon the ether, and that this ether is one vast billowy sea of magnetic light, and is the media of an inner sense of
sight, and the whole mystery is at once cleared up, and the clap-
trap of the charlatans at once exploded and exposed. And thus
this wonderful power is resolved into the mere sensitive ability to
come *en rapport* with this vast ocean of inner light, which may

quite easily be done, as will herein be briefly shown. All that is required is simply patience.

Clairvoyance is the art and power of knowing or cognizing facts, things, and principles, by methods totally distinct from those usually pursued in their attainment. I claim to have reduced it to a system, and to have evolved science from heterogeneity ; to have added new thought, new conception, opened new fields of investigation, and to have discovered the central magnetic law, underlying and subtending the evolutions of somnambulic phenomena, — a brief resumé of which I herewith present.

We are approaching the termination of the first stages of civilization, are bidding farewell to many of its modes, moods, opinions, sentiments, thoughts, and procedures, and are entering upon a new epoch of human history and might, destined to develop powers in man, now latent mainly, but which will yet revolutionize the globe. On earth man is greatest, mind the greatest part of man, and clairvoyance the greatest part of mind. . . . Clairvoyance depends upon a peculiar condition of the nerves and brain. It is compatible with the most robust health, albeit oftenest resulting from disordered nerves. The discovery consists in the knowledge of the exact method *how*, the precise spot *where*, and the proper time *when*, to apply the specific mesmeric current to any given person, in order to produce the **coma** and lucidity. A careful following of the rules herein laid down is generally sufficient to enable the aspirant to attain his or her end.

At the start let it be distinctly understood that fear, doubt, nervous agitation, coarse habits, or bad intent, will retard success, and may prevent it altogether.

When a person cannot be mesmerized through the eye, head, or by reverse passes, success often will follow if the clothes be wet with slightly vinegared water, just over the pit of the stomach and small of the back. If an operator acts, let his left hand cover the rear wet spot, his right the front one, while the gazing process continues as before. REASON : The brain is not the only seat of nervous power ; and we can often reach and subdue it by and through the nerves, nervous matter, and ganglia, situate along and within the backbone. If tractors or magnets are used, their points should be placed just as would be the mesmerizer's hands, and the experiment be continued as before.

At first, clairvoyance, like any movement, nervous or muscular, requires a special effort, but it soon becomes automatic, involuntary, mechanical. KEEP YOUR DESIGN CONSTANTLY BEFORE YOU, AND YOUR SOUL AND INNER SENSES WILL MAKE GROOVES FOR THEM-SELVES, AND CONTINUE TO MOVE IN THEM AS CARS ON RAILS OR WHEELS IN RUTS. Let your groove be CLAIR-*voyance!*

Lucidity is no gift, but a universal possibility common to the human race. (Idiots can and *do* have it.) It is latent, or *still* mind-power, and can be brought to the surface in a majority of cases. *Omnia vincit labor!*

All mental action comes through nervous action, but in these cases the result must be reached outside our usual mental habitudes and paths. The person who attempts to reach clairvoyance, and gets discouraged after a few trials, don't merit the power. If you begin, either by agents or mesmerists, *keep right on.* Every experiment lands you one step nearer success, and that, too, whether you aim at psychometry, lucidity, or any one of the fifty phases or grades of occult power.

Remember that physical conditions influence, modify, and determine mental states, whether these be normal or recondite and mysterious.

Nor forget that pure blood gives pure power. If your blood is foul with scrofula, pork fat, rum, venereal, suspended menses (by nursing, cold, or, perchance, pregnancy), don't attempt clairvoyance till you are free from it. Artists prepare their paints, — you must prepare your body; else no good picture comes, no lucidity follows. Sound lungs, stomach, kidneys, liver, brain, blood, heart, urinal vessels, womb, and pelvic apparatus are not absolute *essentials*, but good preparatives. Above all, the blood *must* be purified, vacated of its poisons, rheums (alkalies, acids in excess), and be toned up to concert pitch, if you would enjoy the music of the spheres, and *know* beyond your outer knowing.

Food, digestion, drinks, sleep, must all be attended to. Mesmeric subjects at first become quite passional, — the devil's bridge. Look out you don't fall through it, for true clairvoyance is coincident only with normal appetites normally sated. Excess destroys it. Every passion, except the grosser, has a normal sphere.

Clairvoyance is qualitative *and* quantitative, like all other mental forces. It is limited, fragmentary, incomplete, in all, because we are all imperfect; *but* no other being can occupy your or my ground, or be so great in our respective directions as we are. No one exactly is like us, — we precisely like nobody. We are like the world, — green spots and deserts,— arid here, frozen there,— fertile in one spot, sterile in another; therefore we should cultivate our *special loves!* Clairvoyant vigor demands attention to the law: "The eternal equation of vital vigor is, Rest equals exercise." Remember this, and retain your power. Clairvoyance is an affair of the air, food, drink, love, passion, light, sleep, health, rest, sunshine, joy, music, labor, exercise, lungs, liver, blood, quite as much as of mesmerism and magnetic coma, for all mental operations are physically conditioned.

Clairvoyance is an art, like any other. The elements exist, but to be useful must be systemized. It has hitherto been pursued, not rationally, but empirically, — as a blind habit, a sort of gymnastics, a means to swindle people, and scarce ever under intelligent guidance like the logical or mathematical or musical faculties of the soul, albeit more valuable than either, and like them, too, subject to the laws of growth. It is far-reaching, and, once attained, though the road is difficult, amply repays the time and labor spent. It has been the study of my life, and that knowledge, which enables me to demonstrate the laws governing it, and by which it may be developed, also enables me to understand and impart those which attend its aberrant phenomena. This mystic ground has hitherto been the prolific hot-bed of a host of noxious, dangerous superstitions and quackeries; and I believe my own is the first attempt to reclaim it to rational investigation.

Clairvoyance is a generic term, employed to express various degrees and modes of perception, whereby one is enabled to cognize and know facts, things, and principles; or to contact certain knowledges, without the use, and independent of, the ordinary avenues of sense. It is produced or attained in various degrees, by different methods, and is of widely diverse grades and kinds, as

A. PYSCHOMETRY, or nervous sensitiveness, wherein the subject does not *see* at all, but comes in magnetic contact with, first, the peculiar material emanations or sphere given off from every person or object in existence, and is analogous to the power whereby a dog finds his master in a crowd, or a hound hunts down a fugitive and pursues him unerringly, from having smelt a garment once worn by that fugitive. By this sense of feeling persons come *en rapport* with others present, distant, dead, or alive, and when the sensitiveness is great, are enabled to sympathetically feel, hence describe, that person's physical, social, moral, amative, and intellectual condition, and, in extraordinary cases, can discern and detect diseases, both of mind, affections, and body, without, however, being qualified to treat or cure said aberrations. Every city in the land abounds with persons claiming to be " clairvoyants," who are not so in any sense whatever, but are, to a greater or less extent, mere sensitives at best; but, in by far the majority of cases, such are rank impostors, fortune-tellers, and charlatans, who eke out a living by dint of a very little good guessing, and a great deal of tall lying. The majority are females of lax principles, who keep a lounge and drawn curtains, — pestilent vampyres, redolent of filth moral, intellectual, and physical, who are loaded with the exuviæ of death, and charge a man or woman with the very vapor of ruin itself.

B. PSYCHOMETRY can be deepened into absolute *perception* by carefully noting the *first* and strongest impressions resulting from contact with a person, letter, or object, and afterward ascertaining the correctness of the verdict come to. A little careful experimentation will develop good results and demonstrate that clairvoyance is an attainable qualification, with proper patience and active effort.

C. INTUITION — the highest quality of the human mind — is latent in most people, developable in nearly all; is trainable, and, when active, is the highest kind of clairvoyance. It is the effortless, instantaneous perception of facts, principles, events, and things. The rule for its promotion is simply, When it tells a tale to test it at once. In a brief time the perceptions will grow clearer, stronger, more full, frequent, and free.

D. The differences between clairvoyance, feeling, or psychometry, and intuition, are these : the first sees, the second feels, the third *knows* instantly.

In our ordinary state, we see through a glass darkly ; in clairvoyance, we see with more or less distinctness ; in psychometry, we *feel* with greater or less intensity, and in intuition, we *leap* to results at a single bound. There are hundreds who imagine they possess one or all of these faculties or qualifications, and arrogate much importance, merely because the ideas have made a strong impression on their minds ; or perhaps they have seen one or two visions or spectral sparks or flashes. Such are what they claim to be, only in the wish. They need training. For clairvoyance is a thing of actual system, rule, and law, and whoever would have it in its completeness or *complexity*, must conform to the *science* thereof, if they expect good results to ensue.

E. The *actual* PERCEPTION is of various kinds and degrees. It does not require brilliant talents for its development, for many seers are inferior morally, organically, spiritually, and intellectually ; yet the higher, more brilliant, and finely constituted a person is, the higher and nobler is the clairvoyance they will develop. Some subjects never get beyond the power to hunt up stolen or lost property ; others stop at the half-way house of telling fortunes ; a number reach the scientific plane, while but a few attain that magnificent sweep of intellect and vision that leaps the world's barriers, forces the gates of death, and revels in the sublime mysteries of the universes. The purer the subject, the better the faculty, is *the* rule. Goodness, not mere knowledge, is power. Remember this !

F. No two persons' clairvoyance is precisely alike. Each one has a *personal idiosyncrasy* that invariably determines his or her specialty, and, whatever that specialty may chance to be, should be encouraged, for in *that* he or she will excel, and in *no* other. The attempt to force nature will be so much lost time and wasted effort. I say this after an experience of twenty years. I had a specialty for the occult, and an early friend, whom I loved tenderly, became unhappy by reason of an accident that, for ten years, rendered him utterly wretched and miserable. He lost all taste for life because of his injury and its effects, and was often tempted to self-murder, and an estrangement sprung up between himself and wife, one of the most beautiful and accomplished ladies in America. A more deplorable wreck was never seen. The wife became morbid, and they used to visit mediums and clairvoyants in hopes of a cure. At that time, 1853, I had a mesmeric subject, and examined for two French physicians in New York, — Drs. TOUTAIN and BERGEVIN. Here I first saw and prescribed for the man, who afterward became my personal friend. Himself and lady were kind to me, and kindness won my undying love. I have had so little of it in this world, have so often been robbed, plundered, and traduced, by so-called friends, that when a real one appeared, I hailed it as the Greeks hailed the sea. We sat one hundred and eighteen times for my friend and his wife, searching for a means of cure, made many costly experiments, and finally was rewarded by a grand discovery.

And so I say to all clairvoyant aspirants, Adopt a *specialty*, and pursue it steadily during your life.

G. When a mesmeric " Circle," self-magnetizing, or (which I do not advise) varied experiment for clairvoyance, bids fair to become a success, and the subject sees flashes, sparks, white clouds, rolling balls of light vapor, or is partially lucid, the tendency of the mind should be carefully noted, and the future direction of the power or faculty be fully decided on, sought for, aimed at, and strictly, persistently, faithfully followed, until a splendid and never-to-be-doubted triumph and success crown your efforts. If you intend to examine and prescribe for disease ; " will-throwing," or read people ; to hunt up lost goods ; detect thieves ; make business examinations, — in short, any special thing ; cultivate that thing and *no other*, else you will spoil your sight, dim your light, and become a sort of Jack-at-all-trades, master of none. You cannot excel in finding lost property, reading the love-life of amorous people, and also describe and prescribe for sick folks. No ; the rule is, One thing, and that thing well. Let the rest alone.

Again ; people are too impatient. They push a somnambule too fast and too far. Be careful, if you look for success. Go short journeys, at a slow pace, if you expect to hold out. While laboring for the French doctors, and others, in New York, I frequently not only examined fifty cases of disease a day, but made all sorts of explorations in as many different directions ; the consequence of which was a chronic lassitude, dyspepsia, angularity, and great irritability of temper, by reason of the unwise step and resultant nervousness.

H. There are various *kinds*, as well as degrees, of clairvoyance : Natural, Intellectual, Medical, Ethereal and Divine, Social, Practical, and purely Mental. Or a clear-seeing of material forms ; lucidity of mind, generally ; lucidity of special cerebral organs ; lucidity upon certain points, — as Medicine, Prevoyance, Religion, Philosophy, Science, Logic, Art, Love, etc. There are many pretenders to all these, nine in ten of whom are rank impostors.

There is a clairvoyance of Introspection, Inspection, and Projection, and these have their appropriate fields in the past, present, and the future; all of which are easily developed and perfected.

There is the common somnambulic or mesmerically induced lucidity. It also comes through the coma or trance, however produced; and yet it is by no means necessary that the patient be fully entranced in order to produce the distinct lucidity. I know capital seers who never were entranced; who never lost their consciousness for a moment. But such cases are far from being common or usual. This first kind of vision exhausts itself on material objects alone, — a mere perception of things without penetrating power. The next stage it reaches is that of mind-reading. In 1853, 4, 5, the writer hereof had this power to a remarkable degree; used to play cards, chess, and read books, blindfold; and this power caused him to be invited to visit Paris, where he exhibited it to the astonishment of the *savans*, and his own glorification. Practically, the thing is useless.

There is a perception, one grade higher than this last, which enables the subject to come *en rapport* with the surface and essence of things, as a tree, man, woman, herbs, etc.; and it grows till the seer beholds and explains somewhat of the penetralia of things; and it culminates in the condition wherein the mind, leaping all the barriers of the outer senses and world, sees and knows things altogether beyond their ranges, and approaches the awful realms of Positive Spirit.

Special cerebral organs become lucid, soon succeeded by an entire illumination of the brain. This is a grand, a sublime, a holy degree; for the subject sees, senses, feels, *knows*, by a royal power; is *en rapport* with a thousand knowledges. A step further, a step inward, and the subject is in harmony with both the upper and lower universes. He or she thenceforth is a POWER IN THE WORLD. All clairvoyants may not claim genius, but all true genius is clairvoyant. Mere talents are dry leaves, tossed up and down by gusts of passion, and scattered and swept away; but Genius lies on the bosom of Memory, and Gratitude at her feet.

I. Very few persons will fail who strictly conform to the general rules here laid down, and fewer still who follow the special plans determined upon. As a rule, I find it safe to declare, that in every one hundred cases seventy-five can become partly lucid; sixty-three can become sensitives; forty-five can reach the second, thirty-two the third, fourteen the fourth, five the fifth, and two the highest degree of clairvoyance their peculiar organization is capable of attaining. Of one hundred men, fifty-six can become seers; of two hundred women, one hundred and eighty can become so.

MAGNETIC CLAIRVOYANCE is that induced by holding the head close to the open horns of a large and powerful horse-shoe magnet. It may be suspended from the ceiling and held to the head lying down, so that when let go it will spring away, or come in contact with its armature (a nail will do) so as to close the circuit. A quartz crystal is nearly as good for this purpose as a horse-shoe magnet; but I prefer a bar magnet to either.

MESMERIC CIRCLES differ from all others, in that to be proper, all who are in one should be insulated; the chairs, and tables, and footstools should rest on glass knobs made on purpose. In these circles, the chances are ten to one that some will go off into the mesmeric coma on the first trial. The circle must wish, will, desire, and favorable results are almost sure to follow. Have patience, if they do not.

NOTE. — All clairvoyants should, to be useful, successful, and enduring, cultivate the *habit of* deep breathing; for all brain power depends upon *lung power*, nor can continued ability exist if this be neglected. All clairvoyants should feed on the best things attainable. Again, all clairvoyants must use great caution in matters of sex. Abstinence is good; totally so, is better, for an error in that direction is fatal to clear vision, or its perpetuity when possessed.

I am told by a friend of mine, in Paris, the best male seer in France, that carelessness in this respect cost him the loss of his vision for a period of seven months. If the party desires to develop sensitiveness only, with a view of becoming a psychometrist, this caution does not apply with such force. If a person was to ask me, is it best to try to be a clairvoyant or a good psychometrist, I should unhesitatingly say the latter, by all means, for it is more easily attained, and, to say the least, is quite as useful, if money-making and tests are the objects sought to be gained.

In all mesmeric experiments, individual or collective, very few become, at first trial, true hypnotic subjects ; and some can never be, owing to peculiarities of organization. The matter can be tested in a variety of ways, — as, for instance, the usual " passes " may be reversed. Or the doubtful subject may look *steadily* at a speck on the wall for six minutes. If drowsy at the end of that time, and the eyeballs have a tendency to roll up, the person *is* a subject, and all that is required is patience. *Or* breathe rapidly, forcibly, for ninety seconds. If it makes you dizzy, you are a subject, and can enter the somnambulic state in any one of a dozen ways. This same operation, often repeated, is almost certain to produce coma ; and if done while lying down, in connection with the horse-shoe magnet operation, will prove successful in enabling the person to see without eyes. In all cases the room should be quite dark. (N. B. — *All* magnetic, odyllic, and mesmeric processes are twenty times oftener productive of grand results if conducted in a dark chamber, than in one lighted artificially, or by the sun. Next to a thoroughly dark room, moonlight is best, and starlight better still.) If, at the end of a few minutes, sparks, flashes, streaks of quick and lingering light are seen, or phosphor clouds float before the face, then one of two things is immediately probable. First, that the party by continuance and repetition can be clairvoyant ; or, second, if not too *scary*, these clouds and sparks may resolve themselves into beatified forms of friends long gone, but unlost.

Forty-eight out of fifty mesmeric experiments fail because the operator wastes, not saves, diffuses, instead of focalizes, the mesmeric force that streams from the eye and fingers. RULES. — Subject and operator must be of opposite sex, temperament, complexion, size, stature, hair, eyes, build, and so on throughout, in order to bring about the best results, without reference to all the talk about positive and negative, which is mostly nonsense ; for I have known a sweet miss only six years old, to thoroughly and effectively mesmerize her great burly uncle, — a man capable of knocking a bull down with one stroke of his ponderous fist, and who was one of the roughest sea-tyrants that ever trod a quarter deck, and yet the little lady rendered him not only helpless, but clairvoyant, by *repeatedly* manipulating his head while he held her on his lap in his daily calls. She had witnessed a few experiments, *believed* she could do the same, tried it on four times, and accomplished it in great glee on the fifth attempt. But the greatest miracle of all was, that the captain's nature became entirely changed, and to-day a better or a gentler man does not sail out of New York harbor! Concentrate your attention on a single point in the subject's head; keep it there. Do not let your thoughts wander. Gaze steadily at it, and it alone, gently waving *your* head and hands over it from right to left, left to right. Repeat the process at the *same time*, daily, for one hour, till the sleep is thoroughly induced. When it is, and you are perfectly satisfied of the fact, you will be *strongly* tempted to ask questions. *Don't you do it!* Resist it. Deepen the slumber in *seven sittings after perfect insensibility ensues!* The eighth time you may ask a few questions, and but a few. Lead the subject slowly, tenderly, holily, gently along, step by step, one subject at a time, and that subject *thoroughly*, — not forgetting what I have said about " specialties."

J. Persons ambitious to become clairvoyant must not forget that a full habit, amorous pleasures, high living, and mental excitement, all are disqualifications. The entire diet must be changed; the linen often; the skin, especially the head and hair, must be kept scrupulously clean; and, to insure speedy success, the food should be very light; fruit, and tea, coffee, and milk may be freely used; but no chocolate, fat, oysters, pastry, and but very little sugar. Nor should the person fail to think, wish, and will the end aimed at continually. Soft and plaintive music is a capital adjunct.

K. The experiments should always be made at first with but few spectators, in a darkened room; and perfect trust should exist between operator and subject. And here let me state that no woman should allow herself to be mesmerized by a man whose principles she cannot fully trust to, for any man can seduce any woman whom he sits by, in magnetic rapport.

L. For some purposes I prefer the Oriental methods of clairvoyance to the full magnetism of European and American practice. These are: first, the mesmerist places a few drops of ink in a proper vessel; gazes therein himself (magnetizing it), and bids the subject gaze also. Presently, the subject will behold a vision in it, and will see pictures of whatever is desired.

I now give the special method of thorough magnetization. First: Let the room be partly darkened. Let there be a mirror in the north end; let the subject's back be toward that mirror, but take care that he or she sits so that the reflected ray of light (magnetism) from the operator's eye will strike the back of his or her head, the subject receiving the reflected ray, — or, operator, subject, and mirror, forming a triangle, which any school-boy can arrange in a moment. Now the subject sits in a chair fully insulated, the feet being on an insulated stool, and no part of the dress or chair touching the floor. The operator also stands or sits on an insulated stool, and, if he is weak in nervous force, should be fully charged with electricity, or from a battery. If spectators are present, seat them silently in the south, east, and west, but not a soul in the north. No silk, not even a cravat, must be allowed in the room. If a piano is there, let some soft and tender chord be played; but take care not to play more than that one on that evening. Previous to the experiment, two magnets have been suspended, one north pole up, the other down, so as to embrace the subject's head without much pressure; the poles must antagonize, and a current will be sent entirely through the head. *Now be careful.* You have already prepared a magnet, or magnetic bar, and when the subject is seated, and the magnets arranged, the operator looks steadily at that point of the looking-glass, whence the reflected ray will glance off and strike the back of the subject's head, just between the fork of the northern magnet, and while doing so he points the bar magnet directly toward the open *neck* of the subject. In a few minutes there ought to be perfect magnetic slumber, and frequently the most surprising clairvoyance exhibited. It is still better if all the spectators grasp a cord on which a copper and iron wire has been bound, the ends being fastened to a chair, so that they point directly to the subject's body. If these directions be faithfully observed, success will follow nine times in every ten experiments.

I may also observe that a slight alteration will render this circle unequalled for different purposes. In such cases let all sit round a table itself, the chairs and stools being wholly insulated. If the room be darkened, you may and probably will have curious mental phenomena. But I advise the chord to be played all the time till results sought for are obtained. Again, let a person sit facing the south, insulated, with the magnets in contact as before, — the person being alone, — and the results desired are almost certain to follow. But let me here say that no one in or out of a circle can reach good and speedy results unless perfectly and absolutely clean. The bath is the very best of preparations for these experiments, and cannot be neglected with impunity. I have known many successes and some failures in conducting all of the above experiments both in this country, England, and France, and I give it as my deliberate opinion that no one need fail in them, and will not, unless their own folly and *impatience* ruin all.

All phantasma are based upon the eternal fact, that whatever exists is something; that thoughts are things, that spirit is real substance, that all things photograph themselves upon other surfaces; that sensitives can see and contact these shadows, lights, • impressions, and images, — as abundantly demonstrated by Baron Von Reichenbach in his researches into the arcana of chemism, light, force and magnetism; also by thousands of others in all lands, and especially wherein it is said disbodied people project an image of themselves upon paper, the artist sketching the outline with a pencil, thus producing pictures of the dead, recognizable by all who ever saw them when walking in flesh and blood. Now, the fact that dead people can and do project images of themselves upon the retinas of sensitives, upon the aura that surrounds certain people, upon similar emanations from houses (haunted !), so plainly that hundreds can see them clear as noonday, is so firmly established that few are so hardy as to deny what is thus, upon the testimony of millions, in all ages, absolutely and unequivocally demonstrated.

It is equally well established, however fools may sneer, that for ages men of the loftiest mental power have used various agents as a means of vision, either to bring themselves in contact with the supernal realms of the ether, or to afford a sensitive surface upon which the attendant dead could, can, and *do*, temporally photograph whatever they choose to, or conditions permit.

During my travels through Africa, Egypt, Turkey, Arabia, Syria, and my intercourse with the *Voudeaux* of New Orleans and Long Island, I became thoroughly convinced of the existence of two kinds of magic: one good and beneficent, ruled and governed by the Adonim; the other foul, malevolent, revengeful, lustful, and malignant. They antagonize each other. The one revels in the saturnalia of the passions; the other, the true Rosicrucian, moves in the light-producing SHADOW of the OVER SOUL. In the one, the adept is surrounded by an innumerable host of viewless powers, who lead him on to great ends and power, but finally sap out his life, and utterly ruin and destroy him or her. And this accounts for much of ill seen and experienced by modern sensitives.

The other leads its votaries through the glimmer toward the light, and unfolds at length that FINAL and CROWNING CLAIRVOYANCE, which consists in a clear perception of relations, causes, connecting links, effects, and uses, by far the noblest and highest attainable while embodied, and this it is that I aim to enable others to reach. BUT TAKE NOTICE: THE TRUE CLAIRVOYANT IN THIS SUBLIME DEGREE MOVES AND ACTS ABOVE AND BEYOND THE TEMPESTUOUS REALM OF THE PASSIONS — DEFIES THEIR UTMOST POWER. PASSION DIMS THE SOUL'S BEST VISION. To reach this lofty eminence, the subject's physical system ought to be purified and proper preparation be made. Food, raiment, habits, thoughts, impulses, all must be modified, for it is idle for any one to expect to reach the greatest apex of possible mental power, unless the right kind of effort be first made. It is God's highest gift to individual man, and cannot be had without a struggle. Since the first edition of this little hand-book (originally printed for sixty subscribers, afterward for five hundred more) was printed, several imitations of it have been born into the world of letters, and every one that I have seen, written by persons who have never known what clairvoyance really is; for it is a demonstrable fact that but a very small percentage are really lucid of all the vast throng that claim this divine and superlatively holy power.

The old-time mesmeric processes — not the mere so-called "psychologizing" — Phœbus, what a word! — nor the "biological" manipulations, once in such high repute wherever their "professors" — heaven save the mark! — could procure a hall and a gullible flock of witnesses; but the good old-fashioned mesmeric induction, seems, in these latter singular times, to have come to an almost total stop and failure, for not one in every hundred experiments is a decided success according to the ancient standard of twenty years; ago and the universal complaint and testimony are that as soon as a subject is once fairly inducted into the hypnotic condition, he or she immediately passes from under the mesmerist's control, and either announces a determination to " go it alone," or become the " subject" of some unknown power, at once entering the domain of mediumship, and thenceforth becoming wholly useless in a ·mesmeric point of view. Now, I think there is no real necessity for such a state of things, nor do I believe it would happen were it not that the operator is deficient in the prime elements of resolution and will, — without both of which, the matter had better not be undertaken at all. Another reason for these frequent failures to produce magnetic states and the concurrent powers of lucidity results from the fact that men who mesmerize females become too susceptible to the powers and influences of lust, and during the operation of magnetizing are too full of lascivious imaginings and hopes to pay strict regard to the matter in hand, and hence the subject spurns the control and acts independently, or the invisible forces that hover about incontinently clap a stopper over all, and forthwith veto and annul the whole affair; for which kindly providence they merit and receive my most hearty thanks, and those of all other well-wishers of his kind, here or over there.

Not all invisible onlookers, however, are to be counted in along with seraphs and angels, nor do they always take a subject away from the mesmerist for that subject's good; but it may happen that obsessing forces of the " Voodoo" grades step in to serve their own peculiar ends. People may laugh as much as they please at the idea of wicked, mean, obsessing, tantalizing, tempting beings, or at the old notions of the alchemists and others of that ilk; but my researches and experience tell a far different story. When it is asserted that there is no inner world of mystic forces under the sun; — that there are no mysterious means whereby ends both good and ill can be wrought at any distance; that the so called " spells," " charms" and " projects" are mere notions, having no firmer foundation than superstition or empty air alone, — then I flatly deny all such assertions, and affirm the conclusions arrived at are so reached by persons wholly ignorant of the invisible world about us, and of the inner powers of the human mind. Although I am not called upon here to explain the *rationale*

involved in this special department at full length, yet elsewhere I
have clearly indicated the direction in which they are to be found.
As well tell me that the sun don't rise, as that there are no means
whereby two dissevered persons cannot be brought in contact, or
that methods do not exist by means of which one person can as-
suredly so work upon another as to gain desired ends (of course
said ends ought always to be good, but even if they be evil, the self-
same principle and power exists, and can be easily brought into
active play and power), no matter whether said ends be those of
love, affection, jealousy, revenge, or love of gain, and lust of
power. I have seen too much of that sort of thing in Asia, Africa, France, California, England, Long Island, and New Orleans,
to doubt the evidences of my senses, and the experience of years
of attentive study of this branch of the great magnetic law, to
doubt it. Indeed, so thoroughly convinced was I of the truth, that
I spent years in travel and association with experts in order to become master of the processes and the rather unpleasant secrets of
the lower (as well as of the higher) kind. In New Orleans nothing is more common than for both men and women to employ the
VOUDEAUX to effect contact with loved or desired ones. I have
never known a failure, albeit some experiments of acquaintances
of mine were rather expensive. A man loves a woman and cannot reach her, or *vice versa;* then comes in the voud. I have a
personal story to tell on this head, with living witnesses in Boston, that would convince the most sceptical person living. More
than that: in this matter of sympathetic art I know that a pair of
twin rings, containing each others' hair, one worn by the loved,
the other by the lover, will blend the two in magnetic rapport to
an astonishing degree. The whole thing is magnetic (another
word for magic) ; and so it is also of the " love-powder " business,
for, although most of the charlatans who pretend to deal in them
are conscienceless swindlers, yet it is possible to prepare and
charge certain materials so that they will retain the *nerve aura* of
one person, and impart it to another, kindling up magnetic love
between them, just as a little yeast will leaven a whole barrel of
flour. Again, it will not do to tell me that one person cannot
throw a spell upon another, and affect them favorably, or the reverse, at any distance ! Hundreds are living witnesses to-day of
my public exposure and defiance of the whole tribe of VOUDEAUX

in New Orleans, at the School of Liberty, in 1864-5, and it was from one of the Voudeaux queens (Alice H——n), — and Madame D——s, a victim, that I gained much of my knowledge in these occult points of black magic. I have known it to be practised for purposes of lust, passion, love, revenge, and pecuniary speculation, and always with a strange and marvellous success. Again, we are told that powers of evil guard hidden treasures, and successfully obfuscate and confuse the would-be finders. I believe it; and also believe that said obfuscation can easily be overcome by a timely resort to powers of a higher grade. People are wont to laugh at and deride all this, as superstitious folly and blind credulity, in spite of the fact that the loftiest minds earth ever held, from HERMES TRISMEGISTUS, and the ALCHEMISTS, down the ages, to the last elected members of the SARBONNE, have believed, do believe it, and I glory in being found in such august company, including ALEXANDER of RUSSIA, and NAPOLEON III.

In corroboration of what I have written, I beg leave to introduce, without comment, the following article concerning " Voudooism, — African Fetich Worship among the Memphis Negroes," from the " Memphis Appeal " : —

" The word Hoodoo, or Voudoo, is one of the names used in the different African dialects for the practice of the mysteries of the Obi (an African word signifying a species of sorcery and witchcraft common among the worshippers of the fetich). In the West Indies the word ' Obi ' is universally used to designate the priests or practisers of this art, who are called ' Obi ' men and ' Obi ' women. In the southern portion of the United States, — Louisiana, Alabama, Mississippi, South Carolina, and Georgia, — where the same rites are extensively practised among the negroes, and where, under the humanizing and Christianizing influence of the blessed state of freedom and idleness in which they now exist, and are encouraged by the Freedmen's Bureau, the religion is rapidly spreading. It goes under the name of Voudooism or Hoodooism.

" The practisers of the art, who are always native Africans, are called hoodoo men or women, and are held in great dread by the negroes, who apply to them for the cure of diseases, to obtain revenge for injuries, and to discover and punish their enemies. The mode of operations is to prepare a fetich, which being placed near or in the dwelling of the person to be worked upon (under the

2

doorstep, or in any snug portion of the furniture) is supposed to produce the most dire and terrible effects upon the victim, both physically and mentally. Among the materials used for the fetich are feathers of various colors, blood, dogs' and cats' teeth, clay from graves, egg-shells, beads, and broken bits of glass. The clay is made into a ball with hair and rags, bound with twine, with feathers, human, alligators', or dogs' teeth, so arranged as to make the whole bear a fancied resemblance to an animal of some sort.

"The person to be hoodooed is generally made aware that the hoodoo is 'set' for him, and the terror created in his mind by this knowledge is generally sufficient to cause him to fall sick, and it is a curious fact, almost always to die in a species of decline. The intimate knowledge of the hoodoos of the insidious vegetable poisons that abound in the swamps of the South, enables them to use these with great effect in most instances.

"With the above as introductory, our readers will better understand the following, which we vouch for as strictly true in every particular. Names and exact locality (although we will say that it occurred within a few miles of this city) are withheld at the request of the lady, whom we will call Mrs. A. :—

"Some months since the only child, a little daughter of Mrs. A., who had been left a widow by the war, was taken ill with what was then thought a slow malarious fever. The family physician was called in and prescribed for her, but in spite of his attentions she grew gradually worse, and seemed to be slowly but surely sinking and wasting away. Everything that medical skill could think of was done, but in vain.

"One evening, while Mrs. A. was watching by the bedside of the little sufferer, an old negro woman, who had been many years in the family, expressed her belief that the child had been 'hoodooed.' Mrs. A. was a creole of Louisiana, and, having been from her earliest infancy among the negroes, was familiar with, and had imbibed not a few of their peculiar superstitions. In despair of deriving any benefit from the doctors, and completely baffled and worn out with the peculiar lingering nature of her child's illness, the suggestion of the woman made a great impression on her mind.

"In the neighborhood were two negroes who bore the reputation of being hoodoo men. They were both Congoes, and were a portion of the cargo of slaves that had run into Mobile Bay in

1860 or 1861. As usual with their more civilized professional brethren, these two hoodoos were deadly enemies, and worked against each other in every possible way. Each had his own particular crowd of adherents, who believed him to be able to make the more powerful *grigats*.

"One of these hoodoos lived on or near Mrs. A.'s place, and, although she was ashamed of the superstition which led her to do so, she sent for him immediately to come over to see her child. The messenger returned, and said that Finney (that was the sorcerer's name) would come, but that Mrs. A. must first send him a chicken cock, three conch shells, and a piece of money with a hole in it.

"She complied with his demands, and he shortly afterward appeared with the cock under his arm, fancifully decorated with strips of yellow, red, and blue flannel, and the three conches trigged up pretty much in the same manner. Placing the conches on the floor in the shape of a triangle, he laid the cock down in the centre of it on its side. He then drew his hand across it in the same direction three or four times. On leaving it the cock lay quiet and did not attempt to move, although it was loose and apparently could have done so had it wished.

"After these preliminaries, he examined the child from head to foot, and, after doing so, broke out into a loud laugh, muttering words to himself in an African dialect. Turning to Mrs. A., who was all anxiety, he told her that the child was hoodooed, that he had found the marks of the hoodoo, and that it was being done by his rival (who lived some miles off, although considered in the same neighborhood), and that he (Finney) intended to show him that he could not come into his district hoodooing without his permission.

"He then called the servants and every one about the place up, and ordered them to appear one by one before him. So great was the respect and terror with which they regarded him, that, although many of them obviously did so with reluctance, not one failed to obey the summons. He regarded each one closely and minutely, and asked if he or she had seen either a strange rooster, dog, or cat around the house in the past few days; to which questions they made various answers. The chambermaid, who attended on the room in which the child lay, was one of those who were particularly

reluctant to appear before him or to answer his questions. He remarked this, and grinning so as to show his sharply filed teeth
nearly from ear to ear, he said, 'Ha, gal, better me find you out
than the buckra!'

"This was late at night, and, after making his 'reconnoisance,'
he picked up his conches and the cock, and prepared to go, telling
Mrs. A. to move the little sufferer into another room and bed.
Promising that he would be back early in the morning, he left the
house. At an early hour next morning he returned with a large
bundle of herbs, which, with peculiar incantations, he made into a
bath, into which he placed the child, and from that hour it began
to recover rapidly.

"He, however, did not stop here. He determined to find out
the hoodoo, and how it had been used; so, after asking permission, he ripped open the pillows, and the bed in which the child
had lain, and therein he found and brought forth a lot of *fetiches*
made of feathers bound together in the most fantastic forms,
which he gave to Mrs. A., telling her to burn them in the fire, and
to watch the chambermaid carefully, saying that as they had
burned and shrivelled up, so she would shrivel up. The girl, who
had displayed from the first the most intense uneasiness, was
listening at the keyhole of an adjoining room, and heard these
injunctions. With a scream she rushed into the room, and, drop-
ping on her knees at Mrs. A.'s feet, implored her not to burn the
fetiches, promising, if she would not, to make a clean confession
of her guilt.

"Mrs. A., by this time deeply impressed with the strangeness
and mystery of the affair, was prevailed upon by the entreaties of
the girl, and kept the 'fetiches' intact, and the chambermaid
confessed that she had been prevailed upon by the other 'hoodoo man' to place these fetiches in the bed of the child. She
protested she did not know for what reason, and that afterward
she wished to take them out, but did not dare to do so for fear of
him.

"As soon as the family physician came in, Mrs. A., completely
bewildered, told him the whole affair, showing him the fetiches,
and making the girl repeat her story to him. He, being a practical man, and having withal considerable knowledge of chemistry,
took the bunches of feathers home with him, and on making a

chemical examination of them, he found them imbued with a very deadly poison.

"Meanwhile, he told the affair to two or three neighbors, and getting out a warrant for the arrest of the malignant hoodoo man, they went to the hut to arrest him. The bird had flown, however, and could nowhere be found. Some of the negroes had, no doubt, carried word to him, and he had thought it best to clear out from that neighborhood. The little patient, relieved from inhaling the poison in her pillow and bed, soon got well, and Mrs. A. has now in her possession the fetiches which came so near making her a childless widow.

"It may not be generally known to the public, but it is nevertheless a fact, that these barbarous African superstitions and practices prevail, and are increasing among the 'freedmen,' not only of Memphis and Tennessee, but of all the Southern States. It is the clearest proof of the inevitable tendency of the negro to relapse into barbarism when left to control himself."

So much for Voudooism. I believe this story to be true, for I have myself been a victim to the thing, but the "doctor" who analyzed the stuff, and found "poison," is both a cheat and a sham to hide his utter ignorance. There *was* no poison about it. The whole thing is purely magnetic, as I can demonstrate at will, for I know this thing from end to end, and speak by the card.

But I have already exceeded the limits assigned to this part of my subject, and shall end it with a few words of advice to those who are mesmerized, who mesmerize others, and to that large class of persons who, unable to be put into the magnetic state themselves, or induce the sleep in others, yet have a constitutional tendency towards the occult,— a peculiar idiosyncrasy which admirably adapts them to the investigation of the inner mysteries of existence, — men and women, who have strange prophetic impulses, weird and arabesque dreams — people who feel strange mental depression without any apparent cause ; persons who are strangely warned of impending death or danger, and before whose eyes fiery sparks glitter a moment and then vanish into the deep blank void again,— such persons make splendid seers through the magic crystals of Artefius and Dee, the Japanese crystal globes, and better still, the splendid magnetic mirrors of TRINUE, and the finer ones imported into this country by the Armenian seer, CUILNA VILMARA,—many of which I have used myself, and selected for others. I think I never so deeply regretted the loss of any material object so much as I did the accidental breaking of a splendid first-class Trinue glass, which cost me twenty-five dollars, but which I would not have parted with for ten times that sum; for not only could I see strange scenes upon its charmed magnetic surface, but of the hundreds who have gazed into it, I never knew of but five who could not see curious clouds moving at will, and phantoramas strangely beautiful and interesting, clear as noonday, and brilliant as polarized light! To all these classes of persons I say: 'Your power depends upon your health, cleanliness, freedom from doubt, irritability, and above all, *impatience.* You must, if you would succeed in penetrating the dark pall which hangs between this world and the under and over realms of light, yet mystery, culti-vate firmness of purpose, steadiness of will, persistency in search of the desired end, volume of lung power and clearness of mind. Mystery never opens her dark doors to the impatient seeker, has been the result of all my experience, and that of every true Rosi-crucian that ever lived, from Thoth-Mor, King of Egypt and high priest thousands of years before the birth of the present materialistic phase of civilization, down to Freeman B. Dowd, the selected grand master of the magnificent order. From THOTH in his palaces, three miles square, on the banks of ancient Nile, to Dowd in Davenport, Iowa, in the shores of mightier Mississippi, each and both, and all the links between, will tell the same story, and recount the same experience, that mystery refuses knowledge to the impatient soul!

The persons who seeks for interior light and perceptive power *cannot* obtain it without a trial which tests the perseverance. They must endeavor to secure equable nervous, physical, and mental health; for the "clairvoyance," falsely so called, which results from sickness and morbid states of mind and body, is at best both unsafe and unreliable; but a psycho-vision, such as can without much difficulty be reached through processes herein laid down, and especially by means of a good glass such as VILMARA's, which, in my opinion, maugre all that table-rapping, planchetting, and other objectors may urge, is incomparably a better, more rapid, and infinitely more satisfactory means than any other known on earth to-day, and, if necessary, I could give the names of scores of adepts in their almost daily use. Some may ask the question: "Spiritualism is now an accredited fact; why not, then, depend upon the revelations obtainable from that source, for answers to all questions concerning the interior senses and the invisible worlds about us? What advantage can a person have by pursuing the search in his or her own person?" To which I answer,

First. Not ten per cent. of what passes for spiritual intercourse has a higher origin than the "medium's" mind.

Second. What one sees, feels, hears, is positive proof to him or her. All spiritual communications come second-handed, but the clairvoyant sees *directly* and reaches knowledge by the first intention.

Third. If a person is lucid (clairvoyant), he or she has a secret personal positive power, and need not consult any other authority whatever.

Fourth. "Mediumship" is automacy; a medium is a machine played on and worked by others, when it really exists; but the clairvoyant sees, knows, understands, learns, and grows in personal magnetic and mental power day by day; and while embodied makes the very best possible preparations for the certain and absolute life beyond the grave, which awaits us all when this "fever called living is over at last."

Fifth. Clairvoyance necessarily subtilizes and refines the mind, body, tastes, passions, and tendencies of every one who possesses and practises it.

Virtue is not a myth; Death is; but by clairvoyance the bars of Death are beaten down, and it opens the gates of Glory, to show all doubting souls the light and life beyond. And why die till one's work is done? Is yours? If not, this divine thing will enable you to more effectually accomplish it.

Possession ordereth use. True clairvoyants do not count themselves as altogether of this world, for they are in connection with, and do the work below of the ethereal peoples of the starry skies. By means of this royal road, the true seer or seeress is enabled to read the varied scrolls of human life; frequently to explain the real significance of dreams and visions; examine and prescribe for those who are sick or ailing in body, soul, mind, heart, affections, hope, ambition, love, aspiration, speculation, losses, gains, fears and troubles of every character, healing bodies, minds, souls; scanning by real positive mental vision, not merely the secrets of a man's or woman's lives and loves, and keeping them as wisdom seeds, to grow into good fruitage presently, — but also reaching the perfect comprehension of the sublime fact that organization determines destinies, — which of course begets charity to the ·neighbor and love to all mankind; hence it is possible to foretell events that must inevitably come to pass, either in the general or special plane of an individual's life and experience. There are ever two roads and three choices before every intelligent human being, and clairvoyance alone is competent to decide which is best, for only this magnificent science and power can enable us to reach the penetralium. As a Roscicrucian, I *know* that men ever fail and die mainly through *feebleness* of WILL. Clairvoyance will teach the adept how to strengthen it. The WILL is one of the prime human powers, and it alone has enabled Man to achieve the splendid triumphs that mark all the ages. If it sleep, or be weak, fitful, or lethargic, the man amounts to a mere cipher. If it be strong and normal, there is no obstacle can successfully impede its sway. We know that the sick are healed by its strength; that homes are made happy by its power; that love itself comes to man through its divine agency; that woman can realize her hopes, *in many directions*, through its resistless force; that GOD is WILL, and whoso hath it fullest and finest, most resembleth him! *Steady willing will bring lucidity of vision and of soul!* By it, also, those who love or would, love may find. Especially is this true of that large class who seek the occult, and strongly desire to reach the cryptic light beneath the floors of the waking world, — I mean the sons and daughters of Sorrow, Anguish, and the Light; the loving, unloved ones of the earth; the lonely pilgrims over desert sands; the heart-reft mariners now sailing and surging over the stormy waters of the bitter sea of Circumstance, — for these are the God-sent, and they travel ever the roughest paths. To all such, WILL, and especially Clairvoyance, is a boon, a true friend, saying, " Come unto me, all ye that are weary and heavy-laden, and I will point the road to rest!" — clairvoyance I mean — not automacy In *any shape.*

What a man or woman eats, drinks, is clothed with, inhales, or is surrounded by, has a direct effect upon the entire being. What shall be partaken of or avoided, in order to purify the person, and create the best possible personal conditions? What chemist can answer that question? Who among them all can tell the precise magnetic, electric, or dynamic state of a man at any given moment of his life? Not one. But the clear seer *can* do all that and more! What shall be taken or avoided in order to strengthen the will? the love nature? the flagging appetites and natural passions? the entire nature? principle? courage? ·fortitude? faith? persistence? Mental lucidity alone can reply. Nothing is more certain than that in certain things you have undertaken, disastrous failure has been the result. And why? You cannot tell, but lucidity will enable you to find out, and render you master or mistress of the situation. There are THREE THINGS only that we strive for in this life, as times go, and these are Love, Money, and Position (Power), but we often fail in reaching all or either, only because we are ignorant of the true road to them, as determined by our respective organizations. What but seership can remedy all this?

Again: It may happen with the best of us that we have forfeited love or lost it. That we are stranded midway on the rocks of distrust, jealousy, incompatibility.

Does passion lie smouldering? Do you love, and find that love unreturned? Are you forced to "eat your own heart," and languish all your days and nights in hopeless gloom, as I have in years gone by? Have meddlers destroyed your peace, broken up the dearest and tenderest ties, wrecked you on the hard rocks of life's roughest paths, deserted you, and left you all alone in the terrible trial hour? Have you been wrecked on life's journey, and seek dry and solid footing? Do you seek communion with the dead, and to know the higher magic of Power? Here is Rhodes, and here leap! Hope! Persistence! Is it worth while to know what your faults of character are, and how the defect may be remedied? to know the reasons why you fail in many of your undertakings? and what will lead you on to success? If man or woman hath lost hope, and love and passion are smouldering wrecks, is it worth while to know how they may be resurrected from their premature graves? All this true clairvoyance will instruct you how to accomplish.

"Sad, sad, are they who know not love,
 But, far from Passion's tears and smiles,
Drift down a moonless sea, and pass
 The silvery coasts of fairy isles.

"But sadder they, whose longing lips
 Kiss empty air, and never touch
The dear warm mouth of those they love, —
 Waiting, wasting, suffering much.

"But, clear as amber, sweet as musk,
 Is life to those whose loves unite!
They bask in Allah's smiles by day,
 And nestle in his heart by night."

Thus sang Fatima; thus singeth every true soul. Clairvoyance should be cultivated by everybody, and then there would be fewer marriage mistakes.

No curtain hides from view the spheres elysian,
 Save these poor shells of half-transparent dust;
And all that blinds the spiritual vision
 Is pride, and hate, and lust. .

Clairvoyance points the road that all should travel. But to be valuable, it should be healthy. Sydney Smith said a good thing when he remarked : —

"Never give way to melancholy; resist it steadily, for the habit will encroach. I once gave a lady two-and-twenty receipts against melancholy. One was a bright fire; another to remember all the pleasant things said to and of her; another to keep a box of sugar-plums on the chimney-piece, and a kettle simmering on the hob.

"Never teach false morality. How exquisitely absurd to tell girls that beauty is of no value — dress of no use! Beauty is of value; her whole prosperity and happiness in life may often depend on a new gown or a becoming bonnet; and if she has five grains of common sense she will find this out. The great thing is to teach her their just value, and that there must be something better under a bonnet than a pretty face for real happiness. But never sacrifice truth.

"I am convinced that digestion is the great secret of life; and

that character, talents, virtues, and qualities are powerfully affected by beef, mutton, pie-crust, and rich soups. I have often
thought that I could feed or starve men into many virtues and
vices, and affect them more powerfully with the instruments of
cookery than Timotheus could do formerly with his lyre."

The principle applies to clairvoyance (lucidity). Be so healthily, or not at all. Self-mesmerization is a very safe and sure road
if it is a slow process. As a matter of course, every tyro and ex-
perimentalist will not make a grand success, because in too great
a hurry; nor is it to be expected; neither will every one skate
or sing well who tries, until a fair amount of practice shall
enable them to do so; that practice necessarily involving many
failures before the final triumph. Mesmerism, self or foreign, has
been in use as an educator for hundreds of long ages, as is proved
by the sculptures and tablets of Ancient Egypt, Syria, Nineveh,
and Babylon, fashioned by civilized man over forty thousand years
ago, if there be any truth in the archæological conclusions of Botta,
Mariette, Champollion, Lepsius, Rawlings, Leonard Horner, and
Baron Bunsen; and in those ancient days, magnetism and clairvoyance, judging from art relics yet remaining, were, as now, used
practically. Then probably, as now, a large class of learned men
affirmed diseases mainly to spring from bad states of the blood and
organs, totally ignoring what clairvoyance then, as now, asserted,
that they were (and are) frequently the result of deeply hidden
causes, albeit there is some doubt whether they even distantly
glimpsed the recently discovered fact, that every disorder bears its
own *signature* or means of cure, as plainly as its direct symptoms
themselves are apparent; that many diseases that have successfully baffled medical science are due to magnetic disturbances in
many instances, — fairly eluding detection until forced to yield
the secret to clairvoyance; that still other, and many, diseases can
only be accounted for on the doctrine of spores, — already herein
explained; nor, furthermore, were the "learned" ones of that
day, any more than their brethren or class in our own time, probably aware, that at least three-fifths of all the evil in the world —
social, mental, national, religious, physical, and moral, sickness,
agony, and premature death — sprung and spring from troubles,
fevers, colds, and acidities in the love departments of our common human nature, as clairvoyance universally demonstrates be-

yond all cavil, as it also, and it alone, can indicate the universal remedy.

Most people are sick because there's trouble in the *love nature*, and that trouble demoralizes the man or woman, destroys the family compact, and, disorganizing the foundations of society, engenders multitudinous hells on earth, and makes crime abound like locusts in a plague!

No power on earth but true clairvoyance, can either detect the causes at work productive of this domestic inharmony, or suggest the remedy.

But what *is* true clairvoyance? I reply, it is the ability, by self-effort or otherwise, to drop beneath the floors of the outer world, and come up, as it were, upon the other side. We often see what we take to be sparks or flashes of light before us in the night; but they are *not* really what they seem, but are instantaneous penetrations of the veil that, pall-like, hangs between this outer world of Dark and Cold, and the inner realm of Light and Fire, in the midst of which it is embosomed, or, as it were, enshrouded; and true clairvoyance is the lengthened uplifting of that heavy pall. It is not the insane raving of obsession, possession, of a puling sickly somnambule! It is not a lure, to win a man or woman from correct practices, or their ideas and standard of *Virtue*, — the Latin word for strength; it is not a trap to bait one's senses; nor the mere ability to make a sort of twilight introspection of your own or some one else's *corpus;* nor a thing calculated to undermine the religious principles of any human being, nor to sap one's moral nature in any way, or to exhaust the strength. But it is a rich and very valuable power, whose growth depends upon the due observance of the normal laws which underlie it. The price of power is obedience to law. If we would be strong, clearseeing, powerful, the rules thereof must be observed; and the adept and acolyte alike be ever conscious that no earthly fame gained, or place reached, or wealth accumulated, will, or probably can, avail them or any human being, when, passed over the river of death, we take our places in the ranks of the vast armies of the dead, as they file by the Halls of Destiny, past the gates of God. What, then, is clairvoyance? I reply: It is the LIGHT which the seer reaches sometimes through years of agony; by wading through oceans, as it were, of tears and blood; it is an interior unfoldment of native powers, culminating in somnambulic vision through the mesmeric processes, and the comprehension and application of the principles that underlie and overflow human nature and the physical universe, together with a knowledge of the principia of the vast spirit-sea whereon the worlds of space are cushioned. Thus true clairvoyance *generally* is knowledge resulting from experi ment, born of agony, and purified by the baptism of fire.

It may require a special examination in certain cases to determine whether the person is best fitted, naturally, for a sympathist, or psychometer, *truly such* in any one of a thousand phases, or for a clairvoyant in any particular degree. To go blindly to work is but to waste your time and effort to no purpose whatever. If your natural bent, organization, and genius best fit you for one particular thing, it were folly to attempt to force yourself into another path.

Never begin a course of experiments unless you intend to carry them on to certain success. To begin a course of magnetic experiments, and become tired in a fortnight because you do not succeed, is absurd. Mesmeric circles are, all things considered, probably the quickest way to reach practical results in a short time.

In the attempt to reach clairvoyance, most people are altogether in too great a hurry to reach grand results, and in that haste neglect the very means required, permitting the mind to wander all over creation, — from the consideration of a miserable love affair of no account whatever, to an exploration of the mysteries enshrouding the great nebulæ of Orion or Centauri. Now that won't do. If one wants to be able to peruse the life-scroll of others, the *first* thing learned must be the *steady* fixing of mind and purpose, aim and intent upon a *single* point, wholly void of other thought or object. The *second* requirement is, *Think the thing* closely ; and *third, will steadily, firmly*, to know the correct solution of the problem in hand, and then the probabilities are a hundred to ten that the vision thereof, or the PHANTORAMA of it, will pass before you like a vivid dream ; or it will flash across your mind with resistless conviction of truth.

Mechanical or magnetic means may be used to facilitate results, but never by the opiates or narcotics. Lured by what Cahagnet wrote about the use of narcotic agents, and strengthened in the hope by what THEOPHILE GAUTIER, BAYARD TAYLOR, FITZ HUGH

LUDLOW, and various other travellers, wrote regarding the use of one, early in the year 1855, I was led to make two experiments; but may God forgive me for so doing. Nothing on earth could induce me to repeat them, or to suffer others to do so, for I know no possible good, but much of unmitigated evil, *can* result therefrom.

In attempting to gain lucidity, I strongly advise purely magnetical means, either at the hands of a judicious manipulator, or by the means indicated herein. A magnetic bandage worn over the head, with the polar plates either in the front or back head, or covering either temple, may be worn to equalize the currents, and induce the slumber. A most splendid magnetic plate is made here in Boston, not only peculiarly adapted to the above purposes, *but also of infinite value to all* sick persons, especially *females*, and men laboring under *any form of nervous impotentia*. . .

No one with eyes can help seeing the notorious fact that infanticide is becoming quite too common, nor, if he has a heart as it should be, avoid regretting that it is so. Not only does the evil exist among unmarried females, but to a far greater extent among the "married," — as that term is generally understood. Why is this so? The last sad fact, I mean. The answer is all too easily reached. It is because so many married women live, not in the anticipated heaven of wedlock, but in an unmitigated opposite thereof. Women who *love* their husbands, delight in the sweet, fond cares, and deep, full joys of maternity; and happy wives never stain their souls with murder, for such it is, at any stage of actual pregnancy, no matter what sophistry may be called into play to explain the thing away. Such casuistry is of no avail at the bar of final judgment, where God himself is on one side the bar in the shape of a quickened conscience, and a murdered human being on the other. No matter how successful the mother may be in the whirl of life and society, in drowning out the remembrance of the evil deed, there will, as surely as God lives, come a time when before her weeping eyes will flit the phantom shape of her dead baby, and that vision will cling to her for many a long epoch after she shall have crossed the boundaries of time, and entered the wide domain of eternity. How shall this dreadful thing be put to a final stop? I reply, not by preaching and denouncing, nor by holding up the horror to public view, for *that* will *never* stop it. Just at this point Love comes in and says : — All these murders are done because I, Love, do not reign in the household, but Lust has taken *my* place. Four-fifths of the children, dead and living, are begotten of sick mothers, in a storm of lust, by thoughtless fathers, generally just after a family quarrel, by way of "making up" and cooling down the tempest. Husbands are, if anything, more to blame for such a state of things, than are the wives, — *for a loved woman never kills!*

If a man loves a woman, and that woman purposely destroys the babe of her body, even at *any stage* of its career, from inception to maturity, the curse of God and his blight is sure to fall on her and destroy the love between them. He may even encourage her to the act, but still the natural curse impends, and in some way it will surely fall, for God always punishes murder. Tempted woman, remember this!

Let no father of an unwedded woman's babe, be ashamed of his own flesh and blood, but do his best to render it and its mother's life happy and contented, for, in the drama of ages, it may be that in other worlds, that child may link him to the Gods! And let husbands learn that a child is the richest property on earth, — genuine real estate, and all the more valuable when properly organized, which it can never be unless genuine love presided at its incarnation. And let all true men and women join, every-where, in one grand effort, here and now, to *very speedily* establish a refuge for poor women, wherein they shall, free of cant, creed or sect, color or nationality, be provided for in the season of trial, unquestioned, and being thus removed from the awful temptation of fœticide, bring forth their children healthily to, and for, God, and this great MAN-wanting world; and then, when recovered, provide, if need be, for the youngling, and repeating the sweet words of the dear Jesus, say, "Let them who are without sin cast at thee the first stone." "Sister, neither do I condemn thee, go thy way and sin no more!"

Is such an ambition a worthy one? I think so. The day of power to do this thing is near at hand. The pleasant hope is the nursling of long, bitter, and weary years. And lo! when all seemed darkest, the golden sun shone out bright and fairly, and albeit I, like all frail creatures of God's infinite love and mercy, have erred, yet never once from the heart, ever from the head, — angular head, — which the world will one day forget, but, I hope

not the soul behind it, for have never fairly made myself understood. It will not always be so, for,—

> Still the world goes round and round,
> And men their courses run;
> But ever the right comes uppermost,
> And ever is justice done.

And, after all, few if any of us want or ask for pity. Justice is
all that's needed — stern justice ; and when that is truly accorded,
there will be found full many an angel where devils only have
been looked for. I, for one, believe this, and have abounding
lenity towards all people on God's earth, except the SLAYERS OF
THE INNOCENTS.

And now I end my task with a bit of advice, hoping that the
matter of this book, original and selected, may benefit all. To
everybody the poet says, and I repeat : —

> " God gave us hands, — one left, one right;
> The first to help ourselves; — the other
> To stretch abroad in kindly might,
> And keep along a suffering brother.
> Then if you see a sister fall,
> And bow her head before the weather,
> Assist at once; remove the thrall,
> And suffer, or grow strong — together' "

It may chance that you, reader, may have enemies ; and if so,
take my advice — for I have them too, — sap-heads mainly. Go
straight on, and don't mind them ; if they get in your way, walk
round them, regardless of their spite. A man or woman who has
no enemies is seldom good for anything, — is made of that kind of
material which is so easily worked that every one has a hand in
it. A sterling character is one who thinks and speaks what she
or he thinks ; such are sure to have enemies. They are as necessary as fresh air. They keep people alive and active. A celebrated character, who was surrounded by enemies, used to remark,
" They are sparks which, if you do not blow, will go out of themselves." " Live down prejudice," was the " iron Duke's " motto.
Let this be your feeling while endeavoring to live down the scandal
of those who are bitter against you ; if you stop to dispute, you

do but as they desire, and open the way for more abuse. Let them talk; there will be a reaction if you perform but your duty, and hundreds who were once alienated from you will flock to you and acknowledge their error. Keep right on the rough or even tenor of your own way.

Why look back to the past, when you should be gazing forward to the future? why hurry to the old haunts, when you see the whole world hastening the other way? A little generous prudence, a little forbearance of one another, and some grains of charity, might win all to join and unite into one general and brotherly search after truth; could we but forego this prelatic tradition of crowding free consciences and Christian liberties into canons and precepts of men, I doubt not, if some great and worthy stranger were to come among us, wise to discern the mould and temper of a people, and how to govern it, observing the high hopes and aims, the diligent alacrity of our extended thoughts and reasons, in pursuance of truth and freedom, but that he would cry out as Pyrrhus did, admiring the Roman docility and courage, "If such were my Epirots, I would not despair the greatest design that could be attempted to make a church or a kingdom happy." Have you faith in the great spirit of our mighty people? Can you discern the instinct of its immortal longing? Do you hope to stem the tide of its irresistible advance, any more than to take the swallows from the sky and stop their flight toward summer? Is it possible you can believe that tradition will serve for anything but men's couch dreams, or that the shadows of antiquity will stand for the substance of Now? The President, Congress, and Supreme Court of to-day are not, do not mean, the same powers of fifty years ago. We call our Constitution the same; but laws vary in their effect with the tendencies of their administrators, as completely as if they were repealed, or altered in their substance. Public opinion consigns some to the cobwebs of the obsolete; altered views change their very interpretation. Are you alone insensible to the change? If not, be up and stirring with the times, — in all affairs, of church, State, politics, labor, love, marriage, and the family; for we live in stirring times, when every one of us must prove ourselves either pieces or pawns in the chess game of life, and to avoid being checked must play WELL!

In these days of turmoil, climatic changes, political change, and revolution, imposture and true revelation, rampant quackery and blooming science, honesty and villany side by side, people may falter and despair of the world and its fortunes; but to do so is to distrust God, and doubt his providence, for he has safely brought us through so far, and therefore let us truly trust him to the end.

Reader, whoever you may be, I beg you to not only read, but *study well*, the glorious meaning of the following sublime jewel from the pen of one of Islam's poets; for once armed with its philosophy you will be impregnable to all assaults, and stand firm amidst the wildest tempest : —

"'Allah! Allah!' cried the sick man, racked with pain the long night through,
Till with prayer his heart grew tender, till his lips like honey grew.
But at morning came the tempter; said, 'Call louder, child of Pain,
See if Allah ever hears, or answers, "*Here am I*," again.'
Like a stab the cruel cavil through his brain and pulses went;
To his heart an icy coldness, to his brain a darkness sent.
Then before him stands Elias: says, 'My child, why thus dismayed?
Dost repent thy former fervor? Is thy soul of prayer afraid?'
'Ah!' he cried, 'I've called so often; never heard the "Here am I; "
And I thought God will *not* pity; will not turn on me his eye.'
Then the grave Elias answered, 'God said, "Rise, Elias, go
Speak to him, the sorely tempted; lift him from his gulf of woe.
Tell him that his very longing is itself an answering cry;
That his prayer, "COME, GRACIOUS ALLAH!" is my answer "HERE AM I!"'
Every inmost aspiration is God's angel undefiled;
And in every 'O my Father!' slumbers deep a 'Here, my child!'"

Women, a last word to you. Perhaps you have a lover or husband, and, that being the case, I say,

If you prize him, let him know it;
If you *love* him, show it, *show it.*

The cure for all wrong and evil is to be found in Clairvoyance, which will enable woman to avoid certain *risks*, at certain times; enable man to understand himself, his wife, and his neighbor; and thus will seership banish crime, and bring peace on earth and good-will among men. So may it be. Let us now turn to another branch of the great subject of seership.

PART SECOND.

THEORY AND PRACTICE — THE MAGNETIC MIRROR.

INTRODUCTORY.

My reasons for writing, compiling, and editing the following extraordinary treatise, — a very difficult task, because wholly out of the ordinary literary channels, — a subject almost wholly unknown to the great majority of readers, and a labor that necessitated very extensive reading and research of and among

"Many a quaint and curious volume of forgotten lore " —

were threefold: First, to relieve myself of the pressure of correspondence on the subject of the treatise, and occult matters generally, by recording the principal points upon which inquiries are made of me, from the fact that I am generally supposed to be thoroughly versed in many of those subtle sciences which for ages have constituted the special studies of the fraternities Pythagorean and Rosicrucian, to which I have, for many years, had the honor and privilege to belong. The second motive was that of obliging one who, in the dark hour of sickness, proved to me a friend indeed; and, thirdly, because the time had come wherein to at least partially ventilate a much misunderstood and tabooed subject, especially as the opportunity was afforded me just then to avail myself of very rare and unusual facilities for obtaining information on the subjects treated of, from one of the first masters of occult science now on the globe in flesh and blood and bone — I allude to the famous Armenian Philosopher, Cuilna Vilmara, then on a brief visit to the shores of Republican and matter-of-fact America.

Aside from these motives is another: Within these past few years there has grown up a very widespread discontent regarding theories, theorists, and the *real* causes underlying and subtending the strange and varied Psychical Phenomena of the age. Especially is this true with reference to the but little understood, yet in reality vast, science of magnetics, one branch of which the following pages are devoted to. The want was felt for a handbook. That want is here supplied.

Amidst the heavy pressure on my time, health, and vital power, but little opportunity has been hitherto afforded the writer hereof, to give the subject the attention it so richly deserves. The task of bringing its scattered ends together has been imperfectly performed herein perhaps; yet have I fearlessly stripped it of the garb of mystery purposely thrown around it by pseudo-mystics, charlatans, and the rank impostors who abound on all hands, and bring odium and disgrace on a matter whereof they are wholly ignorant.

Mirror-seeing is unquestionably a fact and a science, however some may fail in their efforts to see, and despite the sneers of others who are wise in their own conceit, know nothing whatever of the principia of that which they so glibly deride and condemn, and who have not the kind or quality of brains or mental power possessed by those who are better qualified than they are.

Mirror-seeing is but another mode and phase of clairvoyance; it is the self-same power, reached by a different road, and different processes, but is, and can be, carried to a far greater degree of perfection by many persons, while others totally and wholly fail. And here I strongly advise all to refrain from the expense and trouble of mirror-experimentation, who have no tendencies of an interior magnetic or mesmeric character. But possessing these, it is highly probable that satisfactory results will follow a proper trial.

In the "Master Passion," I promised to make a statement in reference to the Davenport Brothers — so-called mediums. They are not worth the ink. I once wrote a book for them from so-called facts and data which they furnished me, and which I believed were true — as I certainly believed them to be genuine media. I am now satisfied that the data furnished were wholly untrue, and the alleged facts entirely imaginary, — in a word, I believe that the D. B.'s are dead beats; in other words, that they are skilful jugglers, without the slightest real spiritual power about any of their performances, save it be "ardent spirits." I am free to confess that for years the brothers deceived me. I acknowledge the fact. "Why did you not apply certain occult power you are said to possess, to the investigation?" I reply: Never thought of it for a long time; but eventually became convinced it had been better to have done so years ago. But better late than never.

These, then, are my reasons for writing this book.

P. B. R.

.   .   .   .

The famous Dr. Dee, of London, and thousands of others, since and before him too, used a plate of polished cannel coal (which identical plate I have myself seen in the British Museum), and other instrumentalities also, as a means whereby to scan and cognize mysteries otherwise wholly unreachable. Some sturdy matter-of-fact people in these material days, wherein a great deal of pseudo-miracleism is current, along with a very little that is real and genuine, are apt to ridicule and laugh at the idea that a mere physical agent can enable one to penetrate the floors of the waking world, and come up, all brilliant and keen, upon the other side. Such scout the notion that an oval, concave, black-white mirror, or a crystal, or even a splotch of ink in a virgin's hand, are really such instrumentalities; and yet I *know* that such is, *incontrovertibly*, the fact; and there are thousands in this country who can testify to the startling truth of what Dee and others claimed in that regard : —

> What if upon the mirror's face serene
> Your lot in life be written ? What, if its pearly sphere
> Disclose to mortal view the far and dark unseen ?
> This seemeth strange, yet doth to me appear.
> I, far events can often clear preview,
> And in my thrice-sealed, dark prospective glass
> Foresee what future days shall bring to pass.

> There, various news I learn, of love and strife,
> Peace, war, health, sickness, death and life ;
> Of loss and gain; of famine and of store;
> Deceits of husbands, wives; of travels on the shore;
> Of storms at sea; the rise and fall of stocks;
> The market's state; and great commercial shocks;
> Of business speculations; good fortune in the air;
> Of when to stop, or go; 'gainst danger to prepare;
> Of turns of fortune; changes in the state;
> The fall of favorites; projects of the great.

The mystical hath been to me a more familiar face than that of friends on earth. In its solemn school of dim and solitary discipline, learned I the languages of other peopled worlds.

Unquestionably immortality is a truth, sublime as Creation, more solid than the granite hills ; and it has been demonstrated in a thousand ways, physically, by viewless spiritual beings. There have been *true* mediums ; there may be still ; but it is equally certain that scores of heartless tricksters abound, whose business it is to counterfeit these testimonies from the dead. These wretched people thrive, for they are sustained by an unthinking class of believers in spiritualism, who care all for phenomena, nothing for principia. I call them horse-radish spiritualists ; and their name is Legion.

Just so in other departments of occult science. False media and pretended clairvoyants, and what I call "horse-radish spiritualists," abound on all hands, — downright, unreasoning fanatics, else a class of most wretched people who, for the sake of a little pecuniary gain, will not, do not, hesitate in the grossest possible manner to counterfeit true and real, and by their trickery bring odium on *true* spiritualism and genuine seership. In these days a *real* medium or clairvoyant is the marked exception to a very broad rule. Just so is it with crystal and mirror seeing, there being ten false to every single true one in the land. The thing itself is older than any civilization now on the globe, yet nevertheless, like genuine mediumship, is constantly being counterfeited. Indeed, turn whichever way you will, a great and deep-seated discontent prevails in the household of the spiritual faith. It is not so among Rosicrucians, albeit their belief in spirits is as strong as strong can be; not *fanatical* — but *strong*. The people are getting tired of modern spiritualism, for they accept, as I do, its real facts, but discard its jargon and crudities. Interested parties try to hide its blotches, but they *will* show themselves. The reason is that there's too much theorizing and too little religion; too much head, and a great sparseness of heart. Carlyle wrote to a friend of mine that a certain given form of modern spiritualism was the "liturgy of Dead Sea apes." Much of it is; but out of what is good and true in it will, I hope, spring glorious things of heart and hope in the good time coming.

. . . .

Madame George Sand gives an account of the famous Count St. Germain, one of the most remarkable magic-mirrorists that ever lived this side the hills of India, and of whom it was claimed that he had lived for centuries, despite the wear and tear of time, and the surging revolutions of decaying empires : —

"What makes this Count de St. Germain an interesting and remarkable personage, to say the least, in my opinion is the number of new and ingenious claims by which he unravels the doubtful points of the obscurer history of States. Question him about any subject or epoch of history, and you will be surprised to hear him unfold or invent an infinity of probable and interesting things, which throw a new light on what has been doubtful and mysterious. Mere erudition does not suffice to explain history. This man must have a mighty mind and great knowlege of humanity. . . . It is with great difficulty that he can be made to talk of the wonderful things. . . . He is aware that he is treated as a charlatan and dreamer, and this seems to trouble him much. . . . He refuses to explain his supernatural power. . . He has filled Europe with countless strange tales." . . Of Count Cagliostro: "It is well known, when Frederick the Great ordered him to quit Berlin, that he left it, in his carriage, in *propria persona*, at twelve exactly, passing *at the same time through each of the gates;* at least twenty thousand people will swear to that. The guards at every gate saw the same hat, wig, carriage and horses, and you cannot convince them that on that day there were not at least six Cagliostros in the field." That same Cagliostro fashioned and owned a magic mirror, now in Florence, Italy, in which whosoever he permitted to gaze, could, and did, see any three things or persons they desired to, no matter whether living or dead! And thousands as sacredly believe this as they do that two and two make four. Nor is this belief any part or parcel of spiritism, so-called; nor superstition; but it is per-

fectly scientific, the whole thing being of a magnetic nature, — clairvoyance under unusual conditions, and easily formulated exactly, as will be
done before I finish this monograph.   I quote : —

Frederick, the Great, was thus forced to resume his philosophical
serenity without assistance.

He said, " Since we are talking of Cagliostro, and the hour for ghosts
and stories has come, I will tell you one which will show how hard it is
to have faith in sorcerers.   My story is true; for I have it from the person to whom it happened last year."

"Is the story terrible?" asked La Mettrie.

"Perhaps," said Frederick.

"Then I will shut the door; for I cannot listen with a door gaping."

La Mettrie shut the door, and the king spoke as follows : —

" Cagliostro, as you know, had the trick of showing people pictures,
or rather magic mirrors, on which he caused the absent to appear.   He
pretended to be able to reveal the most secret occupations of their lives
in this manner.   Jealous women went to consult him about the infidelities
of their husbands, and some lovers and husbands *have learned a great deal
about their ladies' capers.*   The magic mirror has betrayed mysteries of
iniquity.   Be that as it may, the opera-singers all met one night and
offered him a good supper and admirable music, provided he would perform
some of his feats.   He consented, and appointed a day to meet Porporino,
Conciolini, the Signora Astrua, and Porporina, and show them heaven or
hell, as they pleased.

" The Barberini family were also there.   Giovonna Barberini asked to
see the late Doge of Venice, and as Cagliostro gets up ghosts in very good
style, she was very much frightened, and rushed completely overpowered
from the cabinet in which Cagliostro had placed her, *tete-a-tete* with the
doge.   La Porporina, with the calm expression which, as you know, is so
peculiar to her, told Cagliostro she would have faith in his science, if he
would show her the person of whom she then thought, but whom it was
not necessary for her to name, for if he was a sorcerer, he must be able to
read her soul as he would read a book.

" ' What you ask is not a trifle,' said our count; ' yet I think I can satisfy you, provided that you swear, by all that is holy and terrible, not to
speak to the person I shall evoke, to make no motion nor gesture, to utter
no sound, while the apparition stands before you.'

" Porporina promised to do so, and went boldly into the dark closet.

" I need not tell you, gentlemen, that this young woman is one of the
most intellectual and correct persons to be met with.   She is well educated, thinks well about all matters, and I have reason to know no narrow
or restricted idea makes any impression upon her.

" She remained in the ghost-room long enough to make her companions
very uneasy.   All was silent as possible, and finally she came out very

pale, and with tears streaming from her eyes. She immediately said to her companions, 'If Cagliostro be a sorcerer, he is a deceiving one: Have faith in nothing that he shows you.' She would say no more. Conciolini, however, told me a few days after, at one of my concerts, of this wonderful entertainment. I promised myself to question Porporina about it, the first time she sang at *Sans Souci.* I had much difficulty in making her speak of it, but thus she told me : —

"'Cagliostro has, beyond a doubt, the strange power of producing spectres so like truth that it is impossible for the calmest minds to be unmoved by them. His knowledge, however, is incomplete, and I would not advise you, sire, to make him your Minister of Police, for he would perpetrate strange mistakes. Thus, when I asked him to show me the absent person I wished to see, I thought of my music-master, Porpora, who is now at Vienna. Instead of him, I saw in the magic-room a very dear friend I lost during the current year.'"

"*Peste!*" said D'Argens, "that is more wonderful even than the apparition of a living person."

"Wait a moment, gentlemen. Cagliostro had no doubt but what he had shown was the phantom of a living person, and, when it had disappeared, asked Porporina if what she had seen was satisfactory. 'In the first place, monsieur,' said she, 'I wish to understand it. Will you explain?' — 'That surpasses my power. Be assured that your friend is well, and usefully employed.' To this the signora replied, 'Alas! sir, you have done me much wrong; you showed me a person of whom I did not think, and who is, you say, now living. I closed his eyes six months ago.'" . . .

"All this is very fine," said La Mettrie; "but does not explain how your majesty's Porporina saw the dead alive. If she is gifted with as much firmness and reason as your majesty says, the fact goes to disprove your majesty's argument. The sorcerer, it is true, was mistaken, in producing a dead rather than a living man. It, however, makes it the more certain that he controls both life and death. In that respect, he is greater than your majesty, which, if it does not displease your majesty, has killed many men, but never resuscitated a single one."

"Then we are to believe in the devil," said the king, laughing at the comic glances of La Mettrie at Quintus Icilius."

"To conclude. . . . Your Porporina is either foolish or credulous, and saw her dead man, or she was philosophical, and saw nothing. She was frightened, however."

"Not so; she was distressed," said the king, "as all naturally would be, at the sight or portrait which would exactly recall a person loved, but know we shall see no more. But if I must tell you all, I will say, that she subsequently was afraid, and that her moral power after this test was not in so sound a state as it was previously. Thenceforth she has been liable to a dark melancholy, which is always the proof of weakness or disorder of our faculties. Her mind was touched, I am confident, though she denies it."

. . . "And I confess I am under the influence, if not under the power of Cagliostro. Imagine, that after having promised to show me the person of whom I thought, the name of whom he pretended to read in my eyes, he showed me another. Besides, he showed me a person as living, whom he did not know to be dead. Notwithstanding this double error, he resuscitated the husband I had lost, and that will ever be to me a painful and inexpressible enigma."

"He showed you some phantom, and fancy filled up the details."

"I can assure you that my fancy was in no respect interested. I expected to see in a mirror some representation of Maestro Porpora, for I had spoken often of him at supper, and while deploring his absence, had seen that Cagliostro paid no little attention to my words. To make his task more easy, I chose in my mind the face of Porpora, as the subject of the apparition, and I expected him certainly, not having as yet considered the test as serious. Finally, at perhaps the only moment in my life in which I did not think of the Count, he appeared. Cagliostro asked me when I went into the magic closet, if I would consent to have my eyes bandaged, and follow him, holding on to his hand. As he was a man of good reputation, I did not hesitate; but made it a condition that he would not leave me for an instant. 'I was going,' said he, 'to address you a request not to leave me a moment, and not to let go my hand, without regard to what may happen, or what emotion you may feel.' I promised him; but a simple affirmative did not suffice. He made me solemnly swear that I would make no gesture nor exclamation, but remain mute and silent during the whole of the experiment. He then put on his glove, and having covered my head with a hood of black velvet, which fell over my shoulders, he made me walk about five minutes without my being able to hear any door opened or shut. The hood kept me from being aware of any change in the atmosphere, therefore I could not know whether I had gone out of the room or not, for he made me make such frequent turns, that I had no appreciation of the direction. At last he paused; and with one hand removed the hood, so lightly that I was not even aware of it. My respiration having become more free, he informed me that I might look around. I found myself, however, in such intense darkness that I could ascertain nothing. After a short time, I saw a luminous star, which at first trembled, and soon became brilliant before me. At first, it seemed most remote; but, when at its brightest, appeared very near me. It was produced, I think, of a light which became more and more intense, and which was behind a transparency. Cagliostro made me approach the star, which was an orifice pierced in the wall. On the other side of that wall I saw a chamber, magnificently decorated, and filled with lights regularly arranged. This room, in its character and ornaments, had every air of a place dedicated to magical operations. I had not time, however, to examine it, my attention being absorbed by a person who sat before a table. He was alone, and hid his face with his hands, as if immersed in deep meditation. I could not see his features, and his person was disguised by a costume in which I had hitherto seen no one. As far as I was able to remark, it was a robe or cloak of white satin, faced with purple, fastened over the breast with hieroglyphic gems, on which I observed a rose, a triangle, a cross, a death's-head, and many rich ribbons of various kinds. All that I could see was that it was not Porpora. After one or two minutes, this mysterious personage, which I began to fancy a statue, slowly moved its hands, and I saw the face of Count Albert distinctly, not as it had last met my gaze, covered with the shadows of death, but animated amid its pallor, and full of soul in its serenity; such, in fine, as I had seen it in its most beautiful seasons of calm and confidence. I was on the point of uttering a cry, and by an involuntary movement crushing the crystal which separated him from me. A violent pressure of Cagliostro's hand reminded me of my oath, and impressed me with I know not what vague terror. Just then a door opened at the extremity of the room in which I saw Albert; and many unknown persons, dressed as he was, joined him, each bearing a sword. After having made strange gestures, as if they had been playing a pantomine, they spoke to him, in a very solemn tone, words I could not comprehend. He arose and went towards them, and replied in words equally strange, and which were unintelligible to me, though now I know German nearly as well as my mother tongue. This dialogue was like that which we hear in dreams, and the strangeness of the scene, the miracle of the apparition, had so much of this character, that I really doubted whether I dreamed or not. Cagliostro, however, forced me to be motionless, and I recognized the voice of Albert so perfectly that I could not doubt the reality of what I saw. At last, completely carried away by the scene, I was about to forget my oath and speak to him, when the hood again was placed over my head and all became dark. 'If you make the least noise,' said Cagliostro, ' neither you nor I will see the light again.' I had strength enough to follow him, and walk for a long time amid the zigzags of an unknown space. Finally, when he took away the hood again, I found myself in his laboratory, which was dimly lighted as it had been at the commencement of this adventure. Cagliostro was very pale, and still trembled, for, as I walked with him, I became aware of a convulsive agitation of his arm, and that he hurried me along as if he was under the influence of great terror. The first thing he said was to reproach me bitterly about my want of loyalty, and the terrible dangers to which I had exposed him by wishing to violate my promises. ' I should have remembered,' said he, ' that women are not bound by their word of honor, and that one should forbear to accede to their rash and vain curiosity.' His tone was very angry.

" Hitherto I had participated in the terror of my guide. I had been so amazed at Albert's being alive, that I had not inquired if this was possi-

ble. I had even forgotten that death had bereft me of this dear and precious friend. The emotion of the magician recalled to me that all this
was very strange, and that I had seen only a spectre. My reason, however, repudiated what was impossible, and the bitterness of the reproaches
of Cagliostro caused a kind of ill-humor, which protected me from weakness. 'You feign to have faith in your own falsehood,' said I, with
vivacity; 'ah, your game is very cruel. Yes; you sport with all that is
most holy, even with death itself.'

"'Soul without faith, and without power,' said he, angrily, but in a
most imposing manner. 'You believe in death, as the vulgar do, and yet
you had a great master — one who said: " *We do not die. Nothing dies;
there is nothing dies.*" You accuse me of falsehood, and seem to forget
that the only thing which is untrue here is the name of death in your im-
pious mouth.' I confess that this strange reply overturned all my thoughts,
and for a moment overcame the resistance of my troubled mind. How
came this man to be aware of my relations with Albert, and even the
secrets of his doctrine? Did he believe as Albert did, or did he make use
of this as a means to acquire an ascendency over me?

" I was confused and alarmed. Soon, however, I said that this gross
manner of interpreting Albert's faith could not be mine, and that God, not
the impostor Cagliostro, can invoke death, or recall life. Finally, convinced that I was the dupe of an inexplicable illusion, the explanation of
which, however, I might some day find, I arose, praising coldly the *savoir-
faire* of the sorcerer, and asked him for an explanation of the whimsical
conversation his phantoms had together. In relation to that he replied,
that it was impossible to satisfy me, and that I should be satisfied with
seeing the person calm, and carefully occupied. 'You will ask me in
vain,' added he, ' what are his thoughts and actions in life. I am ignorant
even of his name. When you desired and asked to see it, there was
formed between you two a mysterious communication, which my power
was capable of making able to bring you together. All science goes no
farther.'

"'Your science,' said I, 'does not reach that far even; I thought of
Porpora, and you did not present him to me.'

"'Of that I know nothing,' said he, in a tone serious and terrible. ' I do
not wish to know. I have seen nothing, either in your mind, or in the
magic mirror. My mind would not support such a spectacle, and I must
maintain all my senses to exercise my power. The laws of science are
infallible, and consequently, though not aware of it yourself, you must
have thought of some one else than Porpora, since you did not see the
latter.'"

" Such is the talk of madmen of that kind," said the princess, shrugging
her shoulders. "Each one has his peculiar mode; though all, by means
of a captious reasoning, which may be called the method of madness, so

contrive, by disturbing the ideas of others, that they are never cut short, or disturbed themselves."

"He certainly disturbed mine," said Consuelo; "and I was no longer able to analyze them. The apparition of Albert, true or false, made me more distinctly aware that I had lost him forever, and I shed tears.

"'Consuelo,' said the magician in a solemn tone, and offering me his hand (you may imagine that my real name, hitherto unknown to all, was an additional surprise, when I heard him speak it), 'you have great errors to repair, and I trust you will neglect nothing to regain your peace of mind.' I had not power to reply. I sought in vain to hide my tears from my companions, who waited impatiently for me in the next room. I was more impatient yet to withdraw, and as soon as I was alone, after having given a free course to my grief, I passed the night in reflections and commentaries on the scenes of this fatal evening. The more I sought to understand it, the more I became lost in a labyrinth of uncertainty; and I must own that my ideas were often worse than an implicit obedience to the oracles of magic would have been. Worn out by fruitless suffering, I resolved to suspend my judgment until there should be light. Since then, however, I have been impressionable, subject to the vapors, sick at heart, and deeply sad."

. . . "You are about to tell me that he died during the conclusion of the marriage ceremony. I will, however, tell you that he is not dead, that no one, that nothing, dies, and that we may still have communion with those the vulgar call dead, if we know their language and the secret of their lives."

. . . "While waiting for the miracles which are about to be accomplished, God, who apparently mingles in nothing, who is *eternal silence*, creates among us beings of a nature superior to our own, both for good and evil — angels and demons — hidden powers. The latter are to test the just, the former to ensure their triumph. The contest between the great powers has already begun. The king of evil, the father of ignorance and crime, defends himself in vain. The archangels have bent the bow of science and of truth, and their arrows have pierced the corslet of Satan. Satan roars and struggles, but soon will abandon falsehood, lose his venom, and, instead of the impure blood of reptiles, will feel the dew of pardon circulate through his veins. This is the clear and certain explanation of all that is incomprehensible and terrible in the world. Good and evil contend in higher regions which are unattainable to men. Victory and defeat soar above us, without its being possible for us to fix them. . . . Yes; I say it is clear that men are ignorant of what occurs on earth. They see impiety arm itself against fate, and *vice versa*. They suffer oppression, misery, and all the scourges of discord, without their prayers being heard, without the intervention of the miracles of any religion. They now understand nothing; they complain, they know not why. They walk blindfolded on the brink of a precipice. To this the Invisibles impel them, though none know if their mission be of God or of evil, as at the commencement of Christianity, Simon, the magician, seemed to many, a being divine and powerful as Christ. I tell you all prodigies are of God, for Satan can achieve none without permission being granted him, and that among those called invisibles, some act by direct light from the Holy Spirit, while to others the light comes through a cloud, and they do good, fatally thinking that they do evil."

. . . "A few rare persons have the power of commanding their ideas in a state of contemplative idleness, which is granted less frequently to the happy in this world than to those who earn their living by toil, persecution, and danger. All must recognize this mystery as providential, without which the serenity of many unfortunate creatures would appear impossible to those who have not known misfortune."

. . . " She then went to a rich toilette — a table of white marble sustaining a mirror, in a golden frame, of excellent taste. Her attention was attracted by an inscription on the upper ornament of the mirror. It was: *'If your soul be as pure as yon crystal, you will see yourself in it always — young and beautiful. But if vice has withered your heart, be fearful of reading in me the stern reflection of moral deformity.'* "

. . . " *If the thought of evil be in your heart, you are unworthy of contemplating the divine spectacle of nature; if your heart be the home of virtue, look up and bless God, who opens to you the door of a terrestrial paradise.*"

The loftiest spiritualism the world ever saw — that of ancient Jewry — recognized the truth of such mirrors, for they — the "Urim and Thummin"-polished breast-plates — were used for purposes of a celestial divination, and are still so used to-day. Even many of the modern spiritualists recognize the same truths, for their papers frequently contain articles on crystal-seeing, and the magical uses of various jewels and precious stones; while one of their noblest "Psalms of life" contains this beautiful verse : —

> "But most the watching angels guide the thought,
>   If in the mortal's heart be wrong or error,
> Soon by the pure and viewless influence taught,
>   He sees his wrong as in a *Magic Mirror !* —
> He sees the end where leads the tortuous path, —
>   Its darkness and its dangers; and, awaking,
> He finds within his soul a holier faith,
>   And turns, with willing heart, his sin forsaking."

The chief Rosicrucian of all England says, in his recent work on "Fire," "When the mind is surrendered up, as a clear glass (or in, and to it), — *shows of* the magical world roll in." Again: "The gauge is according to the amount of absorption out of this world — flights which the intelligence takes into the worlds not about us. . . We are as the telescope

In the perfect sight-making of the optic glasses — in the focus of his glasses of sense. *But there are other landscapes.* . . and new sights float over, and through, the man-perspectives, and, in new adjustments of the preternatural soul-sight, new worlds are penetrated to, or, which is the same, undulate, centrically, to us, from out the universal flat of shows. Basis of the Rosicrucian secret system, and of all true mysticism or occult knowledge, it is the only thing *possible*. . . . We can glow, by working, as by heavy strokes upon our nature, as like iron in a forge. And this, with an exalting light, forced out — the Immortal fire — wealth — out of another world, even to grow visible to men's mortal eyes. This is ecstasy, and the Divine Illumination. None the less real, because we see nothing of it in the world. Else we should be, as the Bible says, Gods. . . . It is in this magical world of God's light, that sainthood becomes possible, and that the solid world and the exterior nature obey the God-like nature, — worked and drawn, magically, into the circle of its power, . . . by the all-compelling magnetism. Trodden of the spirit. . . . It is a God-instinctive, magic life, in which unliving things are, really, taken to live. . . . The first magician, who is as such recorded, and who gave distinct teachings on the subject of magic, is Zoroaster. The genius of Socrates, Plotin, Porphyrius, and Iamblichus, of Chichus and Scaliger and Cardanus, is placed in the first rank, which included inward (or magic) sight. In later times Robert Fludd (1638–53) and the great magnetist and mirror-seer, Paracelsus." We have records of over three thousand grand masters of the art, — all dead; and of scores — all living — right in our land, — ay, within rifle-shot of where these lines are penned. The plane of the mirror is before us, within so few feet or inches; but its lanes lead down the ages, and its roads up the starry steeps of the Infinite. Its field is — the Vastness below, within, above, and around — and elsewhere; but that elsewhere contains all life next off this life — is an immortal factness. . . .

"In ancient times a natural basin of rock, kept constantly full by a running stream, was a favorite haunt for its magical effects. The double meaning of the word *reflection* ought here to be considered, and how, gazing down into clear water, the mind is disposed to self-retirement, and to contemplation deeply tinctured with melancholy. Rocky pools and gloomy lakes figure in all stories of magic: witness the Craic-pol-nain in the Highland woods of Laynchork; the Devil's Glen in the County of Wicklow, Ireland; the Swedish Blokula; the witch-mountains of Italy; and the Babiagora, between Hungary and Poland. Similar resorts, in the glens of Germany, were marked, as Tacitus mentions, by salt-springs.

"It was, really, only another form of divination by the gloomy waterpool, that attracted so much public attention, a few years ago, when Mr. Lane, in his work on Modern Egypt, testified to its success as practised in Egypt and Hindostan. That gentleman, having resolved to witness the performance of this species of Psycho-vision, the magician commenced his operations by writing forms of invocation, to his familiar spirits, on six slips of paper; a chafing-dish, with some live charcoal in it, was then procured, and a boy summoned who had not yet reached the age of puberty. Mr. Lane inquired who were the persons that could see in the magic mirror, and was told that they were a boy not arrived at puberty, a virgin, a black female slave, and a pregnant woman.

"To prevent any collusion between the sorcerer and the boy, Mr. Lane sent his servant to take the first boy he met. When all was prepared, the sorcerer threw some incense, and one of the strips of paper, into the chafing-dish. He then took hold of the boy's right hand, and drew a square, with some mystical marks, on the palm; in the centre of the square he formed the magic mirror, and desired the boy to look steadily into it, without raising his head. In this mirror, the boy declared that he saw, successively, a man sweeping, seven men with flags, an army pitching its tents, and the various officers of state attending on the Sultan.

"The rest must be told by Mr. Lane himself. 'The sorcerer now addressed himself to me, and asked me if I wished the boy to see any person who was absent or dead. I named Lord Nelson; of whom the boy had evidently never heard, for it was with much difficulty that he pronounced the name after several trials. The magician desired the boy to say to the Sultan, "My master salutes thee, and desires thee to bring Lord Nelson. Bring him before my eyes, that I may see him speedily." The boy then said so, and almost immediately added: "A messenger has gone and brought back a man dressed in a black (or, rather, dark-blue) suit of European clothes; the man has lost his left arm." He then paused for a moment or two, and, looking more intently and more closely into the mirror said, "No; he has not lost his left arm, but it is placed to his breast." This correction made his description more striking than it had been without it, since Lord Nelson generally had his empty sleeve attached to the breast of his coat. But it was the right arm that he had lost. Without saying that I suspected the boy had made a mistake, I asked the magician whether the objects appeared, in the mirror, as if actually before the eyes, or as if in a glass which makes the right appear left. He answered that they appeared as in a common mirror. This rendered the boy's description faultless. Though completely puzzled, I was somewhat disappointed with his performances, for they fell short of what he had accomplished, in many instances, in presence of certain of my friends and countrymen. On one of these occasions, an Englishman present ridiculed the performance, and said that nothing would satisfy him but a correct description of the appearance of his own father; of whom he was sure no one of the company had any knowledge. The boy, accordingly, having called by name for the person alluded to, described a man, in a Frank dress, with his hand placed on his head; wearing spectacles; and with one foot on the ground and the other raised behind him, as if he were stepping down from a seat. The description was *exactly true in every re-*

spect; the peculiar position of the hand was occasioned by an almost constant headache, and that of the foot or leg, by a stiff knee, caused by a fall from a horse in hunting. On another occasion, Shakespeare was described with the most minute exactness both as to person and dress; and I might add several other cases in which the same magician has excited astonishment in the sober minds of several Englishmen of my acquaintance.' So far, Mr. Lane, whose account may be compared with that given by Mr. Kinglake, the author of 'Eothen.'

"It may be worth adding, that, in a recent case of hydromancy known to the writer, the boy could see better without the medium than with it; though he could also see reflected images in a vessel of water. This fact may be admitted to prove that such images are reflected to the eye of the seer from his own mind and brain. How the brain becomes thus enchanted, or the eye disposed for vision, is another question. Certainly it is no proof that the recollected image, in the mind of the inquirer, is transferred to the seer, as proofs can be shown to the contrary. When we look closely into it, Nature seems woven over, almost, with a magical web, and forms of the marvellous are rife." . . .

"Are there intelligent things, of which we know nothing, dealing with the world? Is all a wondrous mechanism, a perfect play of solids which proceeds unerringly, and of whose laws the scientific people are the only interpreters? Are there no such things as miracles? Is the progress of things never changed? And, once out of the world, do the departed never return?

"Is all chance? Cannot the future ever be foreseen? Are all the strange matters told us mere fables or inventions? the forgery of the imaginative mind, or the self-belief of the deluded?

"Whence came that fear which has always pervaded the world? How comes it that, in all times, spirits have been believed? Cannot history, cannot science, cannot common sense conjure this phantom of spiritual fear, until it really resolve into the real? Cannot the apparition be laid? Cannot we eject this terror of invisible *thinking* things — spectators of us — out of the world? Nothing is really done until this be done, if it can ever be done. Man is absolutely not fairly in his world, until this other thing is out of it.

"It cannot be done. And why? Because this fear lies buried in the truth of things. Man's interest lies quite the other way of believing it. This dread of the supernatural is the clog upon his boldness — the mistrust which spoils his plans — which interferes with his prosperity — which brings a cloud over the sunshine of his certainties. Man, then, is afflicted with this fearful mistrust, that, after all, perhaps, his *life* may be the 'dream,' and that unknown future (which is filled with those whom he knew) is the 'waking.' Where have our friends gone? Where shall *we* go? Are there well-known faces about us, though we see them not? Are there silent feet amidst our loud feet? And is it possible to come suddenly upon these — ay, and to hear? Miracle, or flash, in the (contrarily-struck) waves of spirit and body." . . .

"Men secretly tremble. But they hide their fears under the supposed defiance and in the boastful jest. In company they are bold. Separately they reflect,'in their own secret minds, that, after all, these things may be true. True from such and such confirmatory surmises of their own; true from, perhaps, some personal unaccountable experiences, or from the assurance of some friend whom they are disposed to believe. But only *disposed* to believe. Modern times reject the supernatural; are supposed to have no superstition. Superstition? When this modern time is full of superstition!

"But, unfortunately, man has restless curiosity; he loves real truth; he solicits that which he can finally depend upon. He would believe if he could. But the evidence of supernatural things is so evasive — so fantastic — so, in one word, unreliable, that he will hold by the ordinary scientific explanations. All mystery, he says, is that only partially known. When that which constitutes a thing is understood, man declares, the mystery ceases. He only finds nature. Unknown nature before — now known nature.

"The faculty of wonder is a gift; by wonder we mean that highest exhaustive knowledge of the things of this world, upon which to set up, or to construct, the machinery of converse with another. By the ladder of the several senses, we climb to the top platform, the general sense. In most men's minds this bridge of intelligence is not stretched. And this knowledge of the supernatural is rejected like precious gems to grasp which there are, literally, no hands. A compliant cowardice, and an ashamed, merely half-belief have pervaded writers who, really, ought to have known better — who believed while they denied." . . .

"We feel a sensation of surprise and shame, that some writers who, out of the secret strength of their minds, and not out of its weakness, saw that there is more in that which is called superstition than meets the eye, should, because they hesitated and were afraid to deal with it seriously, condescend to disparage and to treat it with ridicule. Superstition is degrading; a sense of the supernatural is ennobling. Walter Scott — although from the constitution of his mind he could not fail to be a believer — has surmised and supposed, and apologized for, and toned into, commonplace and explained, until he has resolved all his wonders — we may say, stripped all his truths — into nothing. Will it never be seen that even truth — that is, *our* truth — may be only plausible? Walter Scott's mind was not profound enough for a really deep sense of the Invisible. We greatly doubt whether he had, or by nature could have, the true wise man's sense of the Great Unseen; that which holds this world but as an island in it. Whether, indeed, he did not designedly deal with the marvellous, and chip and pare, amidst his superstitions, and trim all up with the instincts of a romancist, and the eye to a balance in his favor of the

mere worldly man, is a fair suspicion. As a clear-headed, common-sense
man, who in his good nature, and in his admiration of it, wanted to stand
well with the world; as a man who thoroughly enjoyed his life, and possessed an abundance of rich and *marketable* imagination, — as all this, Walter Scott converted superstitions as into his stock in trade. We seriously
mistrust whether, while believing, he did not— to please the world — still
deny; whether in his affected, and even pretendedly laughing, disclaim
ers, he was not secretly bowing, all the time, before the very thing he
thought it allowable to barter. This, if true, was disingenuous, if not
something worse.

"Nearly all the writers who have treated of the marvellous have done
so in the disbelieving vein. It is the fashion to seem to sneer. All of this
acting before the world comes from the too great love of it; arises out of
the fear of that which may be said of us. There prevails a too great com
pliance with convention; too great a meeting of the universal prejudice
Men are too apologetic, even in their faiths. In the face of standards, few
men have the boldness to be singular. Habit dictates our form of thought
as equally as it legalizes our dress. We dreadfully fear the world.

"Other narrators and exponents of the supernatural — though aware
of the always powerfully interesting material which they have at com
mand — instead of being imbued with the strong sense of the latent truth
in them — may be said, indeed, almost with one consent — though longing
to tell — to begin to parade a sort of shame at their revelations. And
pray wherefore? They are already met more than half-way in every sen
sible man's mind. There are few families — nay, there is scarcely an
individual — who has not had something *naturally* unexplainable in his
history. The supernatural tale always finds an echo in every breast.

"Now, if discredited by writers, the 'supernatural' should not be
treated of by them. There are plenty of subjects at which they may play
but that — if they believe any life but their ordinary life — so serious one
If the possibility of the supernatural be believed, and its instances be
accepted, they are bound, as candid men and honest men, to make the
avowal that they believe. The explanations which are frequently offered
of things appearing as supernatural, are greatly more difficult to credit
than the extra-natural matters themselves. They are often infinitely
clumsy. Somewhat roughly examined, they will continually fall to pieces
of themselves. Of some unaccountable things, in fact, nobody credits the
'explanations.' The uncomfortable fact is *got rid of.* The subject is dis
missed, to make way for the next soliciting object. The wonder is given
up as unexplainable. And that is the whole process. This is a very easy
though not a very conclusive or satisfactory, method of disproving. We
suppose we disbelieve." . . .

"We are weary of the jargon whereby strange and unexplainable —
possibly natural — doubtless natural — *phenomena* have been degraded
The history of all unknown things has been thus similar, that at the out

set, they have invariably been invested with the attributes of the magical.
We must carefully guard ourselves from credulity. Such things as these
presumed Spiritual Disclosures have been known in all ages. There is
nothing newer, other than that they have been suddenly and widely
noticed, in these psychologico-magnetic displays — this supposed spiritual
betrayal — this counter-working and false working of the universal tran-
sitive evolvement — these aberrations of polarity. We have an abiding
dislike to, and we cordially dissent from, all this epileptic wandering;
all this convulsive, incoherent, blameworthy — nay, audacious reaching
out at forbidden things. The pampered human mind can run into any
extreme. We, on the contrary, are friends to the solidest and plainest
common sense.

"We apprehend that the explanation of the great majority of the spiritual manifestations — as they are called — may be, that the forceful magnetism with which the world is charged is (in states of excitement) im-
pelled through the medium — probably the stronger through the reflective
VACUITY; and that it undulates *again* outwards, as we see the rings, or
rather the single ring, upon a sheet of water circumvolve from about a
stone suddenly dropped in. The exterior, magnetic, unconscious rings
may become intelligent, from which 'motived circles' — obeying laws of
which we know nothing, or from which invisible walls, come sounds —
vibrates motion. It may be at the intersection of these 'out-of-sense'
circles (which, from the multitude of minds, must be innumerable, though
they are altogether unsuspected) at which are struck all that strange
attraction and repulsion which we call sympathy and antipathy, and in
which are mind-commerce, and all the puzzling *phenomena* of the so-called
spiritual shows. Thus the mind answers to itself. And instead of 'spirit'
having much to do with it, it is mainly the invisible 'microscopical,' 'unnecessary work to the world' of man's own *other nature;* real spirit being
in the majority of cases still as far off as ever, and outside and transcended
of all of it! All the grave gossip and delusion, therefore, of religious communication and of impartments (truly pieced out, in his wild imagination, by the consultant's own convulsive ingenuity) of disembodied indi-
vidualities, must fall to the ground. The *phenomena* are indisputable.
What they are, the scientific world has yet to learn. We seem to fall, in
these things, into a wide field of vital magnetism. And also into mind-
contagion." . . .

"To reduce the question into the narrowest limits — do spirits exist?
Is there anything apart from the solid, the tangible, the senses of man, the
bulk of nature? Can intelligences exist without a body? Is the world
of soul within the world of flesh, or is the world of flesh within the world
of spirit? Which is the real thing, the material or the immaterial? All
the speculation — all the purposes of life may be confined within these
circumscribed bounds. Either this world is all, or it is almost, nothing.
For if the senses are all of the man; if Nature is just the mere solids

which she presents to us; if the course of circumstances is fortuitous; if we are, really, alone in the world; if nothing is believable — and therefore possible — but what is demonstrable; if human reason is everything, and common sense the true guide and the only guide; why, then, — if all that the world tells us be really true, — the sooner we close the account with this outside phantom-world the better! In this case AWAY WITH IT! And away with all the spiritual tales which are told us! The quicker that we realize to ourselves the fact that all of the supernatural — though, possibly, amusing — is all of the untrue, the more conformable it will be to the comfortable exercising of ourselves. We are children otherwise. Why should we frighten ourselves with fairy tales? Why bring over us this damp of the phantasmagoric view of life? We must, surely, be as the rude and ignorant — as the very unlettered — in distressing ourselves concerning this supposed outside watch of which fabulists have found it their interest to tell us. Surely, in this nineteenth century, when exploration has sifted the world, and science has exposed, however admirable, all the watchwork of it; when superstitions have been, even from their last lurking-places, expelled, and when teaching has almost — we are compelled to use the significant word, *almost* — settled things, we can dismiss our belief in this old world-mistaken idea of the reappearance of the dead; of anything which has ceased out of the world. We can get rid of the fear of the preternatural. In one word, supernaturalism is untrue, because nature is true. And because it has nothing of the supernatural in it. All the groping in the world cannot discover a thing that is not there." . . .

"Science-men are kings in their own domain, which is the world of sense. But they are very untrustworthy guides out of it. They can domesticate us very satisfactorily in this world, and can, piece by piece, put the machinery of it into our hand. But they can never give us another. Nor will *their* glance ever arrest one invisible visitant from out another world; nor will *their* sight ever penetrate, for a moment, past that shadowy curtain — which is yet, perhaps, penetrable — which divides the Seen from the Unseen. Let us give Science due honor; but let us not render up to it our hopes of the future, as equally as all of us of the present." . . .

"True magic lies in the most secret and inmost powers of the mind. Our spiritual nature is still, as it were, barred within us. All spiritual wonders, in the end, become but wonders of our own minds.

"In magnetism lies the key to unlock the future science of magic, to fertilize the growing germs in cultivated fields of knowledge, and reveal the wonders of the creative mind.

"Magic is a great, secret, sudden, and disbelieved-in wisdom (out of this world, and its opposite). Reason is a great, public, relied-on mistake (in this world, and the same with it, in its, by man, accepted operations). The one treads down, and destroys the world. The other springs with it, and makes it. Therefore is one the worldlily true and believed. since man makes himself in it, and grows, into his being, in it. And therefore is the other, in the world-judgment, false and a lie, and a juggle, since man is contradicted in it. So says Paracelsus." . . .

"The crystal seers and mirror viewers use their talent in telling love-sick girls their fortunes, and,"—tenscore more such things are said. What of it? God gave all men brains, but some put them to swindling uses. Are brains, *per se*, bad things to possess? Barbers use leaves of literature to wipe their razors on; yet essays nor the art of printing had that end in view. Trunks are lined with sheets of the Bible, but the books were printed to fatten souls upon. "But all people can't success-fully use these crystals and mirrors?" No one knows till they try. A gentleman of Cambridge left me ten minutes ago, who had stopped a little time, while floating down the river of life, at Spiritualists' Island, but grew tired of the fruit,—religious, social, philosophic, and so on, reputed to grow there; just as I did, and thousands more have, and still more thousands do and will; and he owned a very valuable trinue glass. I doubt if America possesses a more splendid seer than that builder of brick houses and philosophical systems! Why? Because the glass en-abled him, by its magnetic fulness, to burst the bondage of a perverse brainism, and reach the streams that flow beneath the senses. That is all.

In April, 1864, Horace H. Day, the famous financier and true philan-thropist, came to my house in Pleasant St., Boston. That morning I had been mirror-gazing, for pleasure's sake, and the doors of the inner worlds had not yet wholly closed; and I distinctly foresaw, and told him, that in September the country would feel a monetary crash. Result,—the "gold panic" of that month, carrying ruin to thousands, and some to sud-den death by self-slaughter. I know one man who forecasts the markets by means of another trinue; he deals in grain, and as the sheaf whicn appears in the glass rises or falls, so *inevitably* will the market. All he wants is capital to buy, or a sensible man to follow his magneto-commercial *ba-rometer*. He will soon have both. I know a woman who never fails to tell correctly all that others want to know. She is getting rich. But I deprecate this sort of thing; it borders close upon a mere prostitution of a divine instrumentality; for, properly used, this agency is not only second to none other for intromissional and psycho-visional purposes, but is liable to not one single objection, which all others are. Drugs, fumes, odors, ethers, mesmerism, all, and each of them, disturb the nervous system, injure the brain, and their effects are all unhealthy and ab-normal; but the mirror is free from all that, and the things, persons, events, and symbols seen, are actual, almost *tactual*,—as clear, plain and distinct as any other plano-diorama, resembling the effects of the *camera obscura*, and no abnormal state is induced; for the seer is wide awake, broadly intelligent, in possession of every sense, in all its in-

tegrity and watchfulness; while at the same time there is no strain whatever upon the brain; no tension of the nerves. In mesmeric lucidity,
the visions rapidly pass away; never again can they be reproduced or
recalled; but, in the mirror, any given face, place, picture of any locality,
or symbolism, can, by an effort of the will, be made to remain fixed, sta-
tionary, and solid, as long as the seer shall elect; besides which, an infinitely greater percentage of persons can successfully use them than can
be effected by any or all combined of the above-specified agencies. There
are also many diverse drugs, and mesmeric modes; but there are only two
sorts of magic mirrors in existence, — the crystalline, which are but of
little use, and of which the polished coal is a sample; besides being exceedingly difficult to obtain, seeing that only coal of a peculiar shade and
grain will answer the purpose; and even then is utterly useless unless of
a size, without crack, difference, solidity or flaw, sufficient to be correctly
ground, shaped, and polished; for the whole thing depends upon the
power of the mirror to attract, and retain upon its surface, the magnetic
fluid thrown from the eyes; on which magnetic surface in all cases the
things seen appear, and not upon or in the surface or substance of the
mirror itself, as is apparently the case; but mostly above and in front of
it. Sometimes, indeed, the seer sees through the mirror, which, in that case,
serves precisely the same ends and uses to the spirit of the out-looker, that
the eye-pieces and object-glasses do to the external senses of the telescopist
and microscopical investigator. In mesmeric vision there is a necessary
and unget-rid-of-able *rapport* and magnetic sympathy between the operator and the subject, which latter is, therefore, quite as likely to give forth
the pictures, images, memories, and fancies of the former, as he or she is
to reveal the actual truth of and from the outside world. "But spiritual or spirits' magnetisms are not so likely to intrude fantasies; and,
therefore, what a *medium* sees *must* be true and real." To which I reply,
— the objections against human magnetism are tenfold stronger against
the spiritual, or the spirits, so-called, even when it is real and true, which
it is not, over once in at least two hundred times; for beyond all cavil,
what passes for spiritual trance is, in the vast majority of cases, either sim-
ulated, delusive, the effect of mental habit, the effect of the physico-
mental influence of the parties present, or the result of a diseased condition of the nerves and brain. But suppose, for argument's sake, a real
and *bona fide* case of spiritual magnetism. How is the medium or by-
stander to know whether the thing seen is a real photograph of the unseen by mortals, or a transcript from the playful fancy of a disembodied
wag or experimenter? The medium cannot tell, because the very term
and service both indicate a person played upon, — an instrument actual in
unseen hands; a machine worked by unknown forces, — a mere automaton,
made to move, do, act and say, at the will of a power of which neither
they or the bystanders know literally anything whatsoever! There is no
standard of comparison. The medium is a nobody in the matter, while

the invisible, and necessarily totally unknown, operator, is all in all! The difference, therefore, between positive seership and mediumship in any form is the difference of a whole species; or that between *hearing* a description of Paris, and *seeing* Paris one's self; that is to say, it is the difference between act and experience, and the merest hearsay. These opinions are based upon over twenty years' experience and observation of both classes of phenomena.

The second class or order of mirrors (the first embracing all the coals, light-colored metallic mirrors, and crystals, none of which are of much worth, as compared with the perfected instrument of the last century, and the present) are those made upon strictly scientific principles as to *form*, in the first place. After innumerable experiments, it was found that upon removing the skull, and slicing the brain of dead human beings horizontally, just above the ear, that all heads of all the human races were shaped *precisely alike*, and that all differences of external contour depended upon the volume of matter on the periphery or outside surface of the brain, — the cortical matter. It was found, also, that the brain, at that foundation-point, was of the same general form or shape as the earth on which we dwell; that is to say, an oblate spheroid, whence, by experiment, it was deduced that such section of a figure, oblately spheroidal, was also the very best possible form of a magic mirror. Such a figure having two mathematically true and absolutely certain *foci*, so that a stream of magnetism being thrown upon one *focus* slid along the surface and returned to the centre of the other focus, from the centre of the fore-brain, thus completing a magnetic circuit, and rendering the portion of brain in the line of contact exceedingly active, by reason of its increased magnetic play and motion of the brain-particles there situate. So much for the *shape*. But experiment also demonstrated that something else was wanted beside the peculiar outline; for if the fluid impinged upon a perfectly plane surface, it would bound back, and the result of its action would be merely the magnetization of the organs in the fore-brain; beside which, much of the fluid would penetrate the surface, and be lost in space. Then a long series of experiments were instituted by different master-chemists, of different scientific lodges, in various parts of the world, to find a substance which would prevent the escape of the refined *vif*,—this extremely subtle, magnetic fluid,—as the sides of a tub prevent the escape of water. Hence, an alteration in the surface-form of the mirror became requisite, nay, wholly indispensable. A point of the very first importance before the application of the proposed insulating material, even if such should be discovered; which, for a long period of time seemed problematical.

If the convex form was used, the fluid — even supposing the retentive material was applied — would *roll off*, like a soap-bubble from a pipe-bowl. If it was convex, the mass of the invisible globe of magnetic aura would roll off at the ends and sides, and hang in a mass *beneath* the mirror, which of course would never do. And now months were spent in that particular research, until at last a concave was adopted for the glass itself; a thin film of gold was placed close to it on the edge of a peculiarly constructed compound concavo-convex frame, made in conformity with the known laws governing the motion of rare fluids, ethers, and gaseous bodies.

The next step was to find an insulating substance, and one having elective, electric and chemical and magnetic affinity to and with the finest form of magnetism known to science and to human experience. It had already been demonstrated that what would insulate and hold electricity was but an open sieve to that same element in its higher forms and modes; hence, recourse must be had to something else. And so experiments were made, separate and combined, with the alkaline metals, Lithium, Sodium, Potassium, and the hypothetical substance, Ammonium, but without complete success. Then came the metals of the alkaline earths, — Magnesium, Calcium, Barium, and Strontium, but without avail. Then experiments were made with the proper earths, — Didymium, Cerium, Lanthanum, Zirconium, Norium, Erbium, Beryllium, Thorium, Yttrium, Terbium, and Aluminum; but still the proper thing was not found. Attention and trial was next turned to the oxidable metals proper, whose oxides form powerful bases, and these are Copper, Uranium, Lead, Cobalt, Zinc, Cadmium, Nickel, Bismuth, Iron, Chromium, and Manganese; but you might as well try to hold sunlight in a basket, as to confine magnetism within walls made of any, or any combinations of these metals. Therefore the next series of tests embraced the oxidable metals proper, whose oxides form weak bases, or acids, namely, Arsenic, Tin, Vandium, Osmium, Niobium, Antimony, Titanium, Molybdenum, Tetherium, Tantalum, and Tungsten: a nearer approach, but still not the thing required, albeit much time, a deal of money, and more patience, had been expended. Then came the noble metals, whose oxides are reducible by heat, namely, Rhodium, Ruthenium, Silver, Platinum, Iridium, Mercury, Palladium, and Gold. Of course the isomorphous groups of substances, embracing Sulphur, Selenium, Chlorine, Cyanogen, Phosphorus, Fluorine, Iodine and Bromine, were also called into play, and a few of them, as some of the others, were found partially, but not wholly, applicable to the purpose sought to be attained, not even by the aid of others of the non-metallic elements, viz., Oxygen, Nitrogen, Carbon, Boron, Hydrogen, and Silicon, albeit it was found that fusible combinations of fifteen of these score or two of substances, associated with Phthalic acid and Paranapthalene, constituted just the thing required, namely, a compound with strong elective and electric characteristics, presenting a perfectly even, white-black surface, and sensitive in the highest possible degree. Of course this substance is very difficult to make, and well it is that such is the case, else the land would be flooded with counterfeit or very imperfectly constructed mirrors. As it is, it is impossible to make them properly in this country,

and only one man ever imports them, and that man is *Cadlua Vilmara,*
from whose lips I am now reporting, in as plain English as I can com-
mand, this exhaustive monograph upon a very difficult subject — for it is
not easy to correctly catch the meaning of a man whose speech is part
English, French, German, Italian, Armenian, and Arabic, and yet by dint
of great patience, chemical information, two linguists, and half-a-dozen
lexicons, I have succeeded in getting the pith and marrow of all he had·
to say, as himself agreed was the case when reading the French translation. Hence, it will be understood that I herewith give the views of this
great master of the subject, as well as, and interspersed with, my own and
others' beliefs and knowledges of the matters under consideration.

.   .   .   .

The man whose experiences are wholly confined to things of the practical every-day life, is a mere shell, floating on the sea, totally ignorant of
the amazing wealths lying scattered beneath the surface, and piled up in
mountains on the ocean floors; for there's more real worlds *under* this
outside life of ours, than human brain can number. Dream-life, so wonderful, vivid, oftentimes strangely prophetic, is but one of these; and
there is a real state even behind that life of Dreams; and we reach its
mystic borders by the mesmeric roads, while we gaze into its very depths
by the mysterious lens I am here writing about. There is no accident,
no chance, only such seem to be to our outer senses; but when the veil-
pall that hangs over the inner senses is removed, we at once glance down
the mystic lanes, and are in the street of chances; hence the future as the
present — and the past is a fact, and all their events *are now!* Wherefore
it is not difficult to foretell what shall be, if we but get beneath the veil
and glance along the floors of the world. God's numbers never change.
They are perpetual Fixedness, — scannable by whoever has the sciences!

Sir David Brewster, albeit he attempts to pervert the account to other
ends, says that, "It can scarcely be doubted that a concave mirror was
the principal instrument by which the heathen gods (disembodied heroes)
were made to appear in the ancient temples. . . . Esculapius often
exhibited himself to his worshippers of Tarsus; and the temple of Engui-
num, in Sicily, was celebrated as the place where the goddesses (disembodied heroines) exhibited themselves to mortals." Iamblichus informs
us that the ancient magicians caused the gods to appear among the vapors
disengaged from fire; and the conjurer, Maximus, terrified his audience
by making the statue of Hecate laugh. Damascius, quoted, in a bad
cause by Salverte, says, In a manifestation (the cause of which, that is,
a magic mirror, ought not to be revealed), . . . there appeared on
the wall of the temple a mass of light which at first seemed to be very
remote; it transformed itself, in coming nearer, *into a face evidently divine*
and supernatural, of a severe aspect, but mixed with gentleness, and extremely beautiful. According to the institutions of a mysterious religion
the Alexandrians honored it as Osiris and Adonis.

The Emperor Basil, of Macedonia, inconsolable at the loss of his son, went to Theodore Santabaron, celebrated for his miracles, who exhibited to him the image of his beloved son, magnificently dressed, and mounted upon a superb charger. The youth rushed toward his father, threw himself into his arms and — *disappeared !* This aerial image was no trick, for even now optics cannot do anything of the sort; but it unquestionably was produced in, or by, and through, a magic mirror. The plea in this case, of imposture, is absurd.

Mr. Roscoe, in his life of Benvenuto Cellini, gives a thrilling account of that famous artist's adventure with spectres raised by magical means, and, what is more to the purpose, neither Roscoe, Brewster, or Smith, pretend to claim that they, the spectres, were mere figments of fancy. On the contrary, all three admit the thing *was real !* True, they attempt to stave off the supernatural conclusion; but do it very lamely indeed, for it is pretended by them that the magic lantern, playing upon volumes of smoke, accounts for the whole terrific affair, totally forgetful of the fact that Cellini's experience took place in the middle of the *sixteenth* century, whereas Kircher did not invent that instrument till a *hundred years later !* The paragraph in italics on page 154, of Smith's edition of "Brewster's Magic," is too puerile and contemptible to merit notice. Such hard-headed people would fain make us believe that all ghostly appearances are phasmas — even that of Jesus after his death; and that all that's knowable *they* know; when, aside from the multitudinous impostures, there are enough real spiritual visitations and visions to base the hopes of a million worlds upon. In no case, whether the objects viewed are physical or mental — as in dreams, etc., is it the eye which sees, but the faculty of consciousness *within* the eye, brain, soul, of the observer; and as man is a spiritual being, it follows that he has a series of inner senses underlying and subtending his external ones, and which series of internal senses are adapted to his natural-born spiritual nature; and all that he requires is a bridge to help him span the thick matter and reach the spiritual ether. This the mirror enables many, though not *all*, to do.

The condition of death is *mental* activity and *physical* quiescence. If the activity can be had without the quiescence of death, our greatest aim — a new avenue or means of knowing — is attained. This is all the mesmerist and the mirrorist claim to achieve; and both have proved and made good that claim in numberless instances.

The spiritual, therefore the substantial reality of all being, is above and beyond the other senses, and it is only either by his rising to it, through the floors of the outer world beneath which he sinks, or by its descent to him, that he can cognize the actualities of that superior world. In either case, if his motive be good, he ascends toward God. If evil, then his account must be rendered for his act.

When a man, his organs of perception, his intelligent principle, is suspended from its matter-bounded exercise; he can enter the domain of the real, through the gates, of the inner senses; catch glimpses of the forward world, and therefore cognize the events not yet born of time, but which are already begotten of God on the body of Necessity; and, therefore, cannot fail of actual outside show, experience, and being. In the interior state he throws open the windows of his soul, and lets in the sunshine and glory of the spaces; hence all true seers can but deprecate the prostitution of Clairvoyance — true, and therefore very rare — to immoral uses; or that of the mirrors to mere fortune-telling, and such like ends; for, although unquestionably these things have been, are, and can be done, with rare and marvellous success and efficiency by their means, yet it is like causing a first-class race-horse to draw a butcher's cart, or, donning rich attire to plough the land. Hence the caution and advice, simply because the mirror is the gate to another world, another field, another department of the " Inside World."

Says one of the master Rosicrucians of England, — a man whose writings on " Fire " rank him high among the true genii of the world of letters, and one from whom I have largely quoted in this monograph, — a man who deservedly occupies a lofty place in the esteem and affection of every true brother of the Arch Fraternity of Rosicrucians, — in his last great work concerning the " Curious Things of the Outside World ": " The Phantasmagoria of real things are revealed to us only when we escape the outer world." In other words, when we elude by mental swiftness these cast-iron, outward-seeming senses of ours; and when we take a God-bath in the rivers that flow by our souls. There is a light of slumbrous beauty beneath this world-light of ours, and the spaces are thronged with aerial intelligences, unseen by material man. They, to him, wait in darkness, but his darkness is theirs and " our " effulgent light, because it illumines the waste of what to him is mystery. That realm is no shadow-country, no phantom-land. It is a country without sound and noise; yet the fulness of melody echoes through its gorgeous halls, and the wingless cherubim are there in effulgent majesty, to guard its mystic splendors; hence, none but true, brave, feeling souls can *wholly enter* therein. It is a regal domain where *our* under life is topmost. Gautama Buddha, seer of all seers of the olden time, and equalled only now, if ever, tried, to stupid man, these sublime mysteries to reveal; and in that land he has waited six thousand years for the advent of understanders, just as that other king, the lonely Man of Nazareth and Bethlehem, waited nineteen hundred years to find a score of *Christians!* Are they found?

It is only in deep absorption that the soul can outwit the body. Thus, when a man is tempted to waste his manhood in the lap of lust, his senses ever urge him to the deed, albeit he knows it is pollution and death which invite him to the horrid banquet, death-charged and dreadful! But the very instant he sets his soul to gaze upon the temptress, he sees her hollow heart, and realizes the danger to his soul and body; and the sight and the knowledge frees him, that moment, from his thrall; his boiling blood cools; recedes back to its proper channels; his tempestuous passion subsides, and, though weak and exhausted, he still remains a MAN! which is *never* the case when lust extinguishes its fires in the arms of wanton passion. Lo, here, what a truth!

[NOTE. — For an amplification of this thought, see "Love and its Hidden Mystery." Its sequel, "The Master Passion; or, The Curtain Raised." And their antecedent, "After Death; or, Disembodied Man." Also "The Rosicrucian's Story."]

As in the telescope the landscape only is possible, not at either end among the mistakes of the unadjusted glasses, but in the exact focus, where the sight-point is caught, even so we (Rosicrucians) hold that supernatural beings only are possible; visible at that cross-point where the angelic contraction and the magic dilatation intersect. In short, man being himself as the telescope, it is only at the magico-magnetic focus at which the spirit world and the *essential worlds* are to be spied into. Under the dominion of lust, hatred, avarice, *wrong*, no man can enter either! Therefore virtue is its own reward! Divine and supernatural illumination is the only road to absolute truth.

The Platonic philosophy of vision is, that it is the view of objects really existing in interior light, which assume form; not according to arbitrary laws, but according to the state of the mind. This light unites with exterior light in the eye, and is thus drawn into a sensuous or imaginative activity; but, when the outward light is separated, it reposes in its own serene atmosphere. It is, then, in this state of interior repose that all really inspired and correct visions occur. It is the same light so often spoken of in ancient books and modern experiences. It is the light revealed to Pimander, Zoroaster, and the sages of the East. It is Boehmen's Divine Vision or Contemplation; Molinos' Spiritual Guide, and the inner life of all true men — few, — and women — many. (It is the FOUNDATION-FIRE upon which all things whatever are builded; ambushed everywhere; bursting out when least expected; slumbering for ages, yet suddenly illuminating an inebriate's brain, so that he shall see the moral snakes and larvæ of his perversion assume physical proportion and magnitude to fright him back to temperance, virtue, and his forsaken God!

No amount of merely intellectual quickness, sharpness, or solidity will avail the searcher for the unseen! A meek spirit, attention, perseverance, faith open only the doors which lead to the vastitudes.

The world we live in is full of the pattering of ghostly feet, and the music of spiritual singers. It is not difficult to hear them. I may not here write concerning the methods of invocation, because fools will laugh, and the fraternity of the mystical, everywhere, would grieve thereat; and yet it is certain that perfumes, odors, and vapors of magnetic character have, in ages past, and may again and in ages yet to be, proved immense aids to the true seer. There are hundreds who visited the

"Rosicrucian Rooms" in Boylston St., Boston, who marvelled greatly at hearing no raps or ticks, and seeing no clouds pass over the splendid mirror there owned and used, unti¹ perfumes were scattered and incense burned, — whereupon, thousands of patterings rained upon the silver tripod, and glory-clouds, in presence of and seen by scores, floated over the black-sea face of the peerless mirror.

The belief of the supernatural is the only escape out of the coldest infidelity; and the word magic every where is but another term for magnetic, which, being understood, at once removes all its mysteries from the region of the "Black Arts," so-called, into the beautiful realms of ethereal science.

Not every person can see in a mirror of any sort whatever; and hundreds of those who *can* see in them are unable to procure a genuine instrument. To such I recommend a very cheap and beautiful substitute, in the form of a concaved *Claude Lorraine* mirror, easily made, — mould a lump of clay a foot square, *slightly convex.* Dry, and bake it hard, and smooth its surface as perfectly as possible. Then press pasteboard on it till all is smooth and even. Now make another exactly to match it, concave. Between these two place a sheet of fine plate-glass. Bake till it conforms to the required shape. Make two alike. Between these two, cemented one-fourth inch apart, pour black ink till full; seal the aperture left for that purpose, and you have a very good substitute for a magnetic mirror. Else take a glass saucer filled half full of black ink, and you will have as good a mirror as Lane saw so successfully worked in Egypt. A crystal glass of pure water has often served a good purpose to the same end; and, in fact, there are numberless forms of substitutes for the genuine mirror, some of which are very good, but of course not equal to even an ordinary trinue glass. The rules and laws governing these substitutes are precisely the same as those of genuine glasses.

"It will never do to urge that these things lie beyond us. A fruitful source of the spiritual lowness of the modern time is the resolute averting of the face from deep thoughts, which, of course, give trouble. That all the lifting of the mind, that all the sublimest speculation, that all the occupancy of the thoughts by these intensely noble and refining investigations; that all these high ideas, and great ideas, about God's providence, and his purposes in the world, end, when pushed to answer, just where they began — that is, where they first opened, and in no wise attaining to definite result — this is, of course, as true as that men cannot help their speculations and their wonder. But we unconsciously pass higher, and become something better, in such thoughts. We teach ourselves to place the world at a distance. We grow spiritualized; and the very amount of our pleasures multiplies, because it purifies. The fault of the ˙time is haste — is conceit — is a wilful disregard of the higher truths — is a protesting speed to be back again amidst the business of the world — a cowardly acknowledgment of incapacity to cope with the contemplation of man's possible higher destiny — a hypocritical putting-forward of reliance upon, and acknowledgment of, a beneficent superintending Providence in the abstract. The time is so unenthusiastic, everything is so questioned for its utilities, and all is so toned down to commonplace, that it is the voice of exclamation and *alarm* only that can arouse. To obtain a hearing we must call aloud.

"We are involving ourselves in too many deductions. We are thickening ourselves in our mechanic dreams too much. We are posing ourselves with systems. We are living the heart out of us. We are making very clockwork of the grand intensities of nature. Formalism is becoming as a second nature to us, and our method of living is the translation of the life-long charities into pounds and pence. Even our very fine cases — as we may so, perhaps, too 'curiously' figure it — are growing vastly too fine, vastly too wonderful, and too elaborately wrought for us. Why not be of rougher material, and of mere painted outside — of bulk and not sentiment — of the coarse, solid components — of wood and of varnish — instead of making up of such exquisite vermilion blood, and of flesh of a marble-like whiteness in the female examples of us? There be something in superb colors, look you! Why, when we are so laboriously casting ourselves as into ingots for the devil's golden Hades, should we make all this hypocritical fuss about moral improvement? Surely we might as well become stumps — blocks — turn into dead, hard wood, as mean and unhandsome as Lapland idols, when all our foolish pity, and all our human sympathies, are being most convincingly argued and demonstrated out of us; and when the very affections are strangled — oh, think me not too direct and plain-spoken, my dear, contented, but, perhaps, too compliant reader — like irregular children; those which are only sure to bring their parents into discredit. Children of no town, since they belong not to a town, where money abounds! Owning no love, since they cannot claim affinity with the love of bank-notes!

"We have forgotten the inside of the cup in the burnishing of the exterior. Nor — after all — do we live half our life. Our triumph in the common conveniences of life — spite of our vaunting of our perfection in them — go not great lengths. We can forge an anchor. But we cannot cook a dinner. We can spin thousands of yards of calico in two or three revolutions of a wheel. But we, personally, curve so indifferently, that we can scarcely make a bow. The banks groan with our gold. And yet we have not the knowledge profitably — by which we here mean towards our soul's advantage — to expend a single dollar. In this universal Plutus-conversion, our heads — so to speak — are growing into gold, while our hearts are fast becoming but as the merest blown paper-bag inside of us!

"Is this Dutchlike life of toys and trifles right? Is this all of nature; and all of us? Oh, this wilderness of flowers, and, oh, the eternal forests! Let the mind, for a moment, glance at that inexpressible microcosm — far from the vulgar disturbances of the pavements, and out of sight of the glare of the city — in which are the thin, spiry stalks, in whose invisibly minute veins course up the bright-green blood. What a neglected treasury is this world of ours, in which lie undreamed-of riches for the seeking! Why abandon them all — desireless — to the inviting angels? who stand sentinels upon a Paradise upon which we might enter! Oh, those countless diversities, and forever sumless beauties of nature! Oh — stretching above us — all ye vast fields! Blue as the very ultimate floor of divinity; throbbing with worlds, as through the intensity of an all-exultant, all even *violently* God-declarant life! Oh, all ye thousand visible wonders, that scatter spells, as of the fruitful magic, through all this most invisibly populous universe; this universe, whether of man's mind or of the larger macrocosm! Pronounce, ye that know, whether evil, meanness, or wresting to false purpose — whether aught of bad — should profane a theatre of grandeur so immense? Is not man himself — who ought to be the arch-glory, as the *recognition* of it — but as he would seem so desirous of making himself — the blot upon this excellence, the lie to all this overpowering sublimity? Is he not, himself (to speak to him the language which he may best understand), the *bankrupt* in this myriad of banks, whence thought can — and virtue might — draw their inexhaustible supplies?

"Were gold-ribs the very framework of the world, and were they torn out of their mighty sockets; were even the Genius of its Riches shown, barless and central, throned at the very heart of this so detestably, because so for its material glory, worshipped globe — would the sight (or the possession) match against thine immortal chance? Were the spirit of the material world exposed, in a single revelation, in all his blasting splendors, would — O thou miserably merchandising heart! thou seller of thy seat amidst the star-girt saints! thou wretched contemner of the chance offered thee, for thy salvation, by thy God! — would all this compensate for the averting, for one moment, from thee, of the face of the rulers of thine immortal destinies? Confess, thou mad and besotted man! — avouch, thou less defiant than hypocritical rebel to God's heavenly care of thee! — would thy very hugest heap of dross match in value with the tiniest flower, into whose thirsty cup the heaven-missioned spirit poured his eternal dew? Christening to immortality!

"Boastest thou of thy world, and of thy dignity — in thy science — out of it? Art! — what is art to the reticulation of a fungus? What is it to the fine-spun tracery of the meanest moss? Labor — what is thy labor, that thou shouldst pride thyself upon it — when the whole frame of stars be nightly moved? Pride — why, what a shallow thing is this pride, when to the lily of the field even Solomon, in all his glory, has been declared not equal! What be thy stars and ribbons — thy rings and spots — when, than all, the snake hath more splendid? What be thy braveries, and all thine ingenious adornment, when the summer insect — less than thee the 'painted child of dirt' — surpasseth thee at them? What be thy money, when, with whatever assurance thou reliest upon it, it may not spot for thee, as gold nails, thy final melancholy, and, for thy body, long-lasting house? Hoarder for that day of enjoyment which shall never come to thee, in thy last earthly house, all thy tenfold fences of precious metal useless, art thou content to put-up with most ignoble lead! Thou leavest all thy wealth, all 'thy goods and chattels,' and, for aught thou knowest, thou forfeitest thy very soul; and at that, perhaps, terribly sudden summons, thou stand'st not even solitary! For is there not thy misspent life thee to confront? Thou hast bargained away thine heritage, and hast spent the price. And, now, as that as which to be it hath been thy greatest boast — a good 'man of business' — thou must, in rendering up thyself, perform thine own half of the obligations. If the real law be that life to come be alone purchasable by good deeds — as any lawyer will tell thee, friend, if thou consultest him — thou hast miscalculated the law. In thine own interest's sake, then, better a single virtuous act than a reiteration of money victories! Better, for thee, the prayer of the poor man, and the blessings of the fatherless and of the widow, than a whole shipload of plate, an *avenue* of bowing menials, and a whole court of flatterers! Remember that the reckoning, with thee, must come. Disencumber yourself in time. Perhaps the very 'conveyances of thy lands' may not be contained in that box, in which there will be found, at last, but too much room for the possessor himself!

"Art thou wise — even in this world's sense? Art thou sagacious as to the relative meanings of 'debtor and creditor'? When all the world attesteth that these things which I have written concerning inner worlds and the methods of admission thereto, are true, *shalt* thou, then, persevere in so hopeless a chase of phantoms — of fine false things which flee from thee? Shalt thou, with this knowledge, strain for an imagined good, which, even in thine own hand, melteth? Shalt thou, with all these results which experience avoucheth as imminent, still sleep the sleep of fools? Still, with no alarm, fold the accustomed hands, and acquiesce because we see all the world doing so likewise? Shalt thou waste thy precious hours in the pursuit of those anticipated fine things, which, for all thy knowledge to the contrary, are to prove as daggers to thee? If missing *thee*, perhaps to prove nets to the feet to trip up, or pits of selfishness, or of mistake, into which they shall fall, to those to whom thou leavest thine accumulation! That for which thou canst have no farther use, keep it as tenaciously as thou mightest want! Those that thou fanciest best beloved, may but inherit direct ruin in heiring thy riches. That which might have been as a gold mosaic pavement for thee to walk over in thy lifetime, may, in the sinking under thee in thy final disappearance out of this slippery world, convert as into a devil-trap to thy children!

"Love not money, then, other than 'wisely;' and not 'too well.' Grow back into the simplicity of thy childhood. Time hastens from thee.

Thou, really, hast not that half century which thou proposest to live. Live at once; in leading a new life. Prate not in thy vanity, but get thyself to thy knees, thou foolish man! And confess thyself a very child — ay, more than a child — in the *true* wisdom. Recall thy mind to better things than thy wretched traffic, in which by far too much thou imitatest the muckworm. Make much of the holy affections which, like flowers, heaven hath planted in the mind of thee (if thou, like an ox, wouldst not tread them so daily out with thy brutish feet); and of thy children. Each of thine innocent little children contradicteth thee. Thine own youth is that which the most completely exposeth thy false policy. Think that thou hast but the poorest portion of life in thy present life. Thy widest margin of profit, and thy very mound of bonds and of bank-notes, alike shall prove but clogs — ay, but as tons of dead weight — in the hour when unexpected affliction shall start up before thee, or in that time that thou hast thy real summons out of this world. Chains are wealth — ay, chains of heaviest link; hell-forged, but self-wound in one's unconsciousness of acquisition — of which, for its escape, in the last hour the angels have, perhaps, to free the struggling soul! The blessings of the orphan and of the widow — of the lately down-trodden, of but the now rescued — shall be the wings upon which, in triumph out of thy clay, shalt thou mount to the face of God! Then to thy heart shall penetrate, and to thine ears shall reach, that blessed assurance, welcoming thee within the doors of the eternal places: 'Even as thou didst it to the meanest of these thine earthly brethren, hast thou done it unto me!'

"'The roads of heaven, out of this mere, miserable, transitory man's world — this world of disputes and difficulties, of the struggle, and of the eagerness, to live, but of the compelled and confused haste when death arrests — this place of weariness and discomfort, of — in the real reasons of things — very frequently, the high-placed low, and of the lowly-placed high — the ways, leading beyond those clouds of heaven towards which thou gazest, thou longing man! have not those solid barriers of division, between body and spirit, which thou, sometimes, art taught to believe! Look out into the universe — important as thou thinkest thine own globe — and imagine what innumerable 'mansions' thy 'Father's house' hath! By how many ways may the hope (which may be all of thee) travel into the celestial spaces! By how many natural and ethereal wickets the blessed may, according to their natures, enter! Are not the stars as bright doors, opening into the glory?

"'God called up from dreams a man into the vestibule of heaven, saying, "Come thou hither, and see the glory of my house." And to the servants that stood around his throne he said, "Take him and undress him from his robes of flesh; cleanse his vision, and put a new breath into his nostrils; arm him with sail-broad wings for flight. Only touch not with any change his human heart — the heart that weeps and trembles."

"'It was done; and, with a mighty angel for his guide, the man stood ready for his infinite voyage; and from the terraces of heaven, without sound or farewell, at once they wheeled away into endless space. Sometimes with the solemn flight of angel-wing they fled through Zaarrahs of darkness, through wildernesses of death, that divided the worlds of life; sometimes they swept over frontiers, that were quickening, under prophetic motions, towards a life not yet realized. Then, from a distance that is counted only in heaven, light dawned, for a time, through a sleepy film. By unutterable pace the light swept to *them*, they by unutterable pace to the light. In a moment the rushing of planets was upon them; in a moment the blazing of suns was around them. Then came eternities of twilight, that revealed, but were not revealed. To the right hand and to the left towered mighty constellations, that by self-repetitions and by answers from afar, that by counter-positions, that by mysterious combinations, built up triumphal gates, whose architraves, whose archways — horizontal, upright — rested, rose — at altitudes, by spans, that seemed ghostly from infinitude. Without measures were the architraves, past number were the archways, beyond memory the gates. Within were stairs that scaled the eternities above, that descended to the eternities below. Above was below, below was above, to the man stripped of gravitating body. Depth was swallowed up in height insurmountable, height was swallowed up in depth unfathomable. Suddenly as thus they rode from infinite to infinite, suddenly as thus they tilted over abysmal worlds, a mighty cry arose — that systems more mysterious, worlds more billowy — other heights, and other depths — were dawning, were nearing, were at hand.

" 'Then the man sighed, stopped, shuddered, and wept. His overladen heart uttered itself in tears; and he said, " Angel, I will go no farther! For the spirit of man aches under this infinity. Insufferable is the glory of God's house. Let me lie down in the grave, that I may find rest from the persecutions of the Infinite! For end, I see, there is none." And from all the listening stars that shone around issued one choral chant: "Even so it is! Angel, thou knowest that it is. End there is none that ever yet we heard of." — "End is there none?" the angel solemnly demanded. "And is this the sorrow that kills you?" But no voice answered, that he might answer himself. Then the angel threw up his glorious hands to the heaven of heavens, saying, "End is there none to the universe of God? Lo, also, THERE IS NO BEGINNING!" ' . . .

" If the bond of the whole visible world be the universal magnetism, then the immortal, unparticled Spirit, of which this Magnetism be the shadow, may be that ineffable potentiality in which the real religion shall be, alone, possible. In this manner shall Sainthood be true of all time. In this ' new world of the old world,' shall miracle be possible. In this manner out of the familiar shall come the wonderful. In this angelic medium shall Heaven be! And alone be." . . .

" In my book I have sought to cast loose the chains which men think they have of this dense, solid, soulless world of ours. Ignoring Spirit out of it, as a thing of no account. Rejecting miracle, because it will not submit to a machinery which produces the world; but which is, of course, incompetent to explain the mastership over itself. Which machinery dissolves wholly at the frontier that separates the great, outside, unknown world, from the little, inside, known world.

"Mine is not so much an attempt to restore to Superstition its dispossessed pedestal, as it is to replace the Supernatural upon its abdicated throne.

"And if, after listening, for so long a time, to the mighty eloquence of Saint Paul, when heaping inference on inference and proof on proof concerning the religion of the Redeemer, of which he was then so triumphant a champion, Agrippa breaks up his charmed revery (in which he, himself touches on the confine of conviction) with the astonished exclamation: 'Paul, Paul, thou almost persuadest me to be a Christian!' may we not hope that, now, to the reflecting reader, such light of probability shall shine from our arguments, as that he, too, shall 'almost see' that the Supernatural may be possible about him even in his own familiar hours, and in this our modern and present day?" . . .

"In the work now in the reader's hand, the author proposed to himself these certain objects. First: to the best of his power, to establish the possibility of the supernatural. This science denies. Next, to prove the present existence of the supernatural. This faith rejects. Lastly, to show that all religion is only possible, not in the *thinking* that we believe (which means miracle, *per se*), but in the *actually* believing. For mankind may be divided — in the subject of belief in divine matters, or, rather, in the crediting of anything out of this world — into three great sections. First, into those who believe nothing; secondly, into those who would believe if they could; lastly, into those who *think* that they believe. In this last large class, are included — as to believe impossible things is impossible — all the conscientious and 'good' of all the various orders. People can only believe according to the best of their power; and their common sense stops short of the *conviction* of miracle; in which, as I contend, real religion can alone lie." . . .

"It will only be thoughts which arise out of what the author has said, that will set the reader musing. He will see that there lie other things beyond, farther reference to which in a work of this nature — indeed, in any work — would be improper. Those who will accept, as clear illumination out of the fogs and the delusions of this world, are those who, by intelligence and by knowledge, are fitted to recognize. Ordinary readers, of whom, out of curiosity and the natural vivacity of mind, the author feels assured he will have many, will accept the same pages as most amusing matter, certain things in which will stimulate the profoundest thoughts in those who have the higher gift. For, in reading, there are two views." . . .

" To the guardians of the more recondite· and secret philosophical knowledge, of whom, in the societies — abroad and at home — there are a greater number, even in these days, than the uninitiated might suppose, it will be sufficient to observe that in no part of his book (though every reader will find — it is presumed — abundance of entertainment in it) is there approach, by the author, to disclosures which, in any mind, might be considered too little guarded." . . .

" Respecting the real meaning and purpose of the extraordinary philosophy of the Rosicrucians — some slender portion of which this book contains, as also do all of Dr. P. B. Randolph's works — indeed they are, from first to last, *wholly* Rosicrucian — there is the profoundest general ignorance. All that is supposed of them is that they were a mighty sect, whose acquirements — and, indeed, practice — were involved in so much mystery that the comprehension of them was scarcely possible. And this famous secret society has been not only the problem, but the amusement, and converted into the romance, of modern times. On the principle — usually a very true one — that all of the unknown must, therefore, be imposing, the story of these Cabalists has served the turn of those who sought to impress. If modern writers have made use of their history, it has been to weave up the materials into romance. The name of the Rosicrucians has been a word of might with charlatans; they have been the means of exciting, with the dealers in fiction. The character of the mystic fraternity — its designs and objects — have been a potent charm with all those who thought that they possessed, through it, a power of stimulating curiosity. Members of the Society of the Rosy Cross have been introduced, as heroes, in novels; have mysteriously flitted as the *deus ex machinâ*, through tales of the imagination. From want of knowledge of what they were, they have been supposed everything. They have been wondered at — laughed at — feared — set down as magicians, and as exempted from the common lot of the children of men. Fanaticism, dreaming, imposture, and, in the milder form of accusation, self-delusion; all this has been assumed of them. From the curious forms in which they chose to invest their knowledge; because of the singular fables which they elected as the medium in which their secrets should be hidden, they have been looked upon as quite of another race — as scarcely men. But they have been much mistaken.

" Justice is so late of arrival to all original thinkers — the terms of prejudice, and of astonishment (not in the good sense), are so long in falling off from profound searchers — that, even now, the Rosicrucians — in other words, the Paracelsians, or Magnetists — are totally ignored as the arch-chemists to whose deep thoughts and unrelaxing labors modern science is indebted for most of its truths. As astrology (not the juggles of the stars, but the true exploration, seeking the method of being, and of working, of the glittering habitants of space); as astrology was the mother of astronomy, so is the lore of the Hermetic Brethren (miscalled in only one of their names — and that the popular — Rosicrucians) — the groundwork of all present philosophy. In its applied side, Rosicrucianism is the very science which is so familiar, and so valuable. But as the Hermetic Beliefs are a great religion, they, of course, have their popular adaptation; and, in consequence, there is a mythology to them. There must always be a machinery to every faith, through which it may be known. And the mistake of people is in accepting the childish machinery and the coarsely (but fitly) colored mythology of a religion for the religion itself, and all of it. Hence the Rosicrucians' supposed doctrine of the invisible children of the various elements; its sylphs or sylphids, its kobolds, krolls, gnomes, kelps, or kelpies, its salamanders and salamandrines, and its ondines; hence all the picturesque but necessary catalogue of paraded items of belief, to constitute it a system that the vulgar might accept as reconcilable with sense. It is surprising that brighter intelligences have not perceived all this as only coverings and concealments. It ought to be seen, at once, that it is not possible to display certain things. Mystics are the chief priests of every religion. For perhaps there never was a worse-founded supposition than that knowledge was for all people. The minds of some classes of individuals never grow. Men who have arrived at the last of their mental possibilities are as much children to the higher intelligences, and are as unfit for their knowledge (which has, however, the great merit of being *sure to be disbelieved*), as the children, knowledge to whom, of higher things than their capacity admits of, we conceal and falsify in nursery talk. All that has, as yet, been disclosed of the beliefs of the Rosicrucians is fable fitted only to the comprehension of those who demanded a *mythos* as the first necessary of a faith. As more and more of the light is kindled in the mind, so is the disciple introduced into the greater and greater truth. As he, himself, becomes fit, so are things fitted to him. And in the mystic sense (and, because it is mystic, the only true sense), when men leave their settled facts and move towards things assumed as unbelievable, they only, by an inverse process, as it were, approach the real facts and' leave their children's stories and fables. Mystical, fantastical, and transcendental — nay, impossible — as the studies and objects of the Rosicrucians seem in the modern ultra-practical days, it is forgotten that the truths of contemporaneous science are all based on the dreams of the old thinkers. Out of natural philosophy, the occult brethren sought the spirits of natural philosophy. And to this inner heaven — so unlike ordinary life — through purifications, through invocations, through humbling and prayers, through penances to break the terms of body with the world, through fumigations and incensing to raise up another world about them, and to place themselves *en rapport* with the inhabitants of it, through the suspension of the senses and thereby to the opening of other senses — to the shutting-out of one state, in order to the passing into another state; to all this the Rosicrucians sought to reach.

" By the Philosopher's ' Stone ' we acknowledge that we mean the magic mirror, or translucent spirit-seeing crystal, in which impossible-seeming things are disclosed. The *menstruum* or universal dissolvent, a transmuting element, the *elixir vitæ* or a power of general regeneration, magical means in their widest sense — a capacity to deal with the materials of nature until quite contrary things are evolved of them; every phase of impossible knowledge has been assumed of these philosophers. That soon, outside of our material nature, the grand lights begin to shine, was their argument. But by the vulgar their accomplishments were suspected as the forbidden golden keys of the very treasure-house in which lie the means of unlocking the gates to the immortal knowledge!

"Those who take up these volumes will see, by what is advanced in this concluding chapter, that they deal with no crude or inconclusive fancies of merely enthusiastic, imaginative, theorizing people. Nor that they are to be defrauded in the unconscientious work, sought to be diverted from solid judgment in the flimsy attractions, nor simply seduced in the plausibilities of the book-making tribe; traitors — compelled or lured — to the great commonwealth of letters!

"The second volume of ' Curious Things ' (by Hargrave Jennings, F. R. C., from which copious extracts have been made herein), in which will be found some very original and interesting speculation, points, as its keynote, as it were, to the following well-supported though surprising assertion: 'That extraordinary race, the Buddhists of Upper India (of whom the Phœnician Canaanite, Melchizedek, was a priest), *who built the Pyramids, Stonehenge, Carnac, etc.*, can be shown to have founded all the ancient Mythologies of the World, which, however varied and corrupted in recent times, were originally ONE, and that ONE founded on principles sublime, beautiful, and true!'

"And at this stage of my book, I may, with propriety, cease addressing in the formal and distant third person, and, in my individual capacity, assure the kind reader (who has accompanied me thus far, and so long) that the volumes upon which he has been occupied have been the full work, in one manner and another,'of two years, I first formed the notion of such a book as this at no less distant a date than nine years; namely, in 1851. It was in October, 1858, that I first commenced upon these volumes. Except a certain interval from December, 1859, until the succeeding March, when I was otherwise occupied, the task has held me, uninterruptedly, down to the present. Twenty years of metaphysics are exhibited in the conclusions of this book. They have, thus, the guarantee of delay and of thought. Much thinking produces good acting." . . .

"Distributed as over the wide and heaving sea of history, most numerous fragments, evidently of a mighty wreck — most wonderful the ship, and of materials and of design portentous and superhuman — have floated as to the thinker's feet. Chips as of strange and puzzling woods — pieces that, dissevered, bore no meaning — contradictory objects — diverse matters, only, through keenness, with suspected relation — a beam, portions of rope, the angle of the prow, Items that, by long guessing, could alone be discovered to have once constituted a fabric; these have been, as it were, gathered up, and built, into a whole Argo, humbly, in my book. And I have sought to reconstruct a majestic ship, and have traced a celestial and the sublimest story, which we have heired, unknowingly, through the ages. Whether I have succeeded in demonstrating the philosophical possibility of the Supernatural, I am not to be the judge." . . .

There are seven distinct magnetic laws, which, when obeyed and enforced, cannot possibly fail of producing given effects or results; and the first of these, and without which but little can be done, either with reference to one's self or another, is PERSISTENCE OF PURPOSE TO A GIVEN END, AIM, AND PURPOSE. My own career is a proof-case in point. Many years ago I made the discovery, elsewhere announced, that most of human ills, social, domestic, mental, and moral, were the result of infractions, by excess, entire continence, or inversion, therefore *perversion*, of the sexual passion and instinct common to the human race. But there was no known cure for those evils, and I was therefore compelled to search for one in the regions of the unknown. With certain speculative and transmitted data to start from, I began, and for long years continued, the investigation of the matter, with a persistence, patient research, and strength of will that shrunk at no obstacle, admitted no possibility of defeat or failure. The result of that persistence is before the world, which this day acknowledges that I have perfected a series of nervo-vital remedials, better than have yet been produced on the globe, to relieve the nervous troubles of mankind, no matter whether they resulted from excess or inversion of the sex-instinct of mankind, or from prodigal waste of life from over-study, sedentary, in-door life, or excessive mental, moral, or nervous toil.

The second law is that of ATTENTION — condensed, steady, concentrated attention to, and upon, the person, object, principle, purpose or thing intended or attempted to be achieved. The exercise of this power will increase the general mental strength, *rapidly*.

The third law is, CALMNESS, quietude! Nothing can be gained by ebullition, hurry, excitement, especially in matters pertaining to seership, by any means whatever, because it destroys the direction and volume of the magnetic currents, and scatters to the winds what ought to be a steady, waving flow of power.

The fourth magnetic law is that of WILL; not persistence in, or of, it; but will itself — the *It*-shall-be-as-I-want-it-power of the soul. It is the central pivot about which all the others rotate, and receive their impulsion toward the ends aimed at.

The fifth law is that of INTENSITY, which needs no explanation. The sixth law is that of POLARITY, — the most important one of all, because without it not much can be done; with it, there is no human being but can be reached and influenced, to a degree perfectly astonishing, as I have demonstrated in a hundred cases, one of which shall serve as a lesson : —

Mrs. A., for instance, having heard that I sometimes give lessons of a psychical character, comes to me with the old story, that her husband's love has grown cool, that he is attracted elsewhere, and she is wretched in consequence, and wants to draw him back by magnetic, or any other equally sure, innocent and certain means. If she already possesses a good magnetic mirror, all the better; if not, I tell her to borrow one from a friend, and use it as hereinafter directed; and I begin by inquiring the height, complexion, color of eyes and hair, approximative weight, and build, and age of her husband. This, to determine his temperament, with *reference to her own.* Suppose she is a blonde and her husband a brunette. These are the proper *relative* temperaments, and such *ought* to be a happy union, and they twain disagreeing, I conclude that the fault is mainly her own. She is, very likely, too cold, exacting, imperious, disobliging, heedless of him; non-caressive; and I tell her to *correct* these faults in herself to begin with, for such a man with such a temperament will be quick, impulsive, passionate, restive, and full of angles; yet, armed with love, the blonde wife can not only subdue him, but win him from any *brunette* woman under the sun. How? Blondes are electric, brunettes magnetic, and very susceptible to influences *steadily* brought to bear upon them. *His* weakest point, and therefore greatest want, is *caressive* love. Let the blonde wife play *that* card, and her game is won; and that's what is meant by Polarity. Let her sit before the mirror, bring up his image before her therein, and when it is steadily fixed before the soul's eye, let her bring all the other six laws to bear upon it — *him* crowning all, as she looks upon him with true, pure, wifely desire; the seventh law, which all understand.

But suppose *both* parties are blondes. It is evident that *caressive* love won't do there, because both are of the same *electric* temperament, and the straying husband, nine chances in ten, has become fascinated with some dark-eyed, dark-haired, olive-hued; passional woman, whose warm, magnetic nature is altogether fascinating, and chains him with bands of triple steel. Well, in that case, the wife must attack him through the door of his higher nature, and prove to him by her steady, unchanging treatment of him, that soul is superior to body, mind to mere beauty, solicitude and interest in his affairs of more worth than whole oceans of mere passionalism. His brain and sense, then, is the *point d'appui* in that case — is the polar point. Reverse the sexes and circumstances, if you choose to do so, yet the law is still the same.

But there is another principle here, that is of equal importance, in all cases where a love-sundering is the result of a third party's intrusion, influence, and power. Repulsion is precisely as powerful as Attraction, and we will suppose that the fault lies neither in the wife nor husband, but in a female rival of the former, who of course is just as susceptible to magnetic influences, hatred, dislike, etc., as any other human being. Well, to illustrate this very important point: Once in Cairo, Egypt, I conversed with an educated Arab on this very topic, and learned that it was a common custom for an injured wife to bring before her the image of the recreant husband — by force of will — frequently using, for want of a better, either a glass of water, or such a magic mirror as is described in Lane's "Modern Egyptians," and in Mrs. Poole's "English Woman in Egypt;" but as there are plenty of Wulees, Kutbs, and dervishes all over Egypt, it is quite an easy matter for such to gain an hour's use of a genuine glass or jewel. In this mirror, no matter whether a common one or a diamond, she invokes the Simulacrum, or magnetic image of the woman who has stolen her husband's affections. "But suppose she don't know who the woman is?" That makes not the slightest difference; all she has to do is to will *the* woman, and no earthly power can prevent her image, wraith, picture, or spiritual form and face from appearing. When she does so: "*Back on thy head, all the misery thou hast heaped upon mine! Back to thy heart the pangs thou hast made me endure!* In the name of love, whom thou hast disgraced; in the name of Him who is omnipotent, I turn the love my (husband or lover) bears thee, into its opposite — dislike and hatred; and in Allah's name I change thy mutual passion into foul disgust and horror. In the name of God so may it be!"

Now your *practical* people will probably laugh at such a method, such means, and yet in so doing they laugh at God, at human love, breaking hearts, and the irresistible magnetic laws of the entire universe of the great Supreme, and I had rather face the "devil" than the solemn prayer of an injured woman; for I *might* escape *his* clutches — if he had any; but it is certain that such a message, from such a woman, under such circumstances, and in such a cause, would find me and fang my soul with horror wherever I might hide; because woman's love is the strongest force on earth; her cause is the purest, strongest, and most just; and all the good powers of the universe are in sympathy therewith. Nor do I believe it possible for a failure to occur, provided the woman be in *dead earnest*, and follows up her blow day by day, till her (magnetic) victory is achieved.

But injured wives are not the only ones in Syria, Egypt, Turkey, and Arabia, who have recourse to magnetic means in love affairs; for widows resort to the identical methods, save only a change of *formulas:* "Gracious Allah, thou hast declared it is not good to be alone; wherefore grant that I may (herein) behold *one* suited to me." This, supposing she has no *special* man for a husband in view. If she has, then she brings up his image, and directs her force upon *him.* I have heard of many successes; I have known of no failures; nor do I see any reason why the white women of Western Europe and North America should not be quite as powerful and successful in these matters as their Arabian and Egypto-Syriac sisters, or the quadroons of the South, who notoriously practise the same things to the same ends. If one of these women has no special man in view whom she desires to have for a husband, then she continues the experiments until a series of psycho-visual phantasmal faces flit across the strange, dark face of the magnetical glass. When one appears toward whom her soul yearns, as only a woman's soul *can* yearn, and she feels toward it as love alone can feel, she holds the simulacrum there, firmly, steadily, brings into active play the law heretofore explained, and forthwith impresses — wherever, whoever, he may be — the living original of that phantom picture, by a magnetism forceful, irresistible. The next thing is to find the man; to bring the two together; and this is done by the same means; for the lucidity has often revealed localities, places, names. Seldom, however, is there a case like the above; for generally the woman already knows of the man she wants, and then her object is to inspire him, and the meeting afterward is a very easy affair.

Of course this whole thing is nothing but clairvoyance, pure and simple, entirely magnetic from first to last, only that it is Oriental, instead of Western, and is reached by methods differing from those in practice by Europeans and Americans generally — if we except a few of the Wandering Zingaras, and Southern Octoroons.

In gazing into the profundities of the magnetic world through the agency of a mirror, it sometimes happens that very strange things are seen; as a hundred letters from mirror-seers to me most unequivocally demonstrate. Occasionally an eye, emblematic of the very loftiest seership and celestial guidance, is beheld, and blessed indeed are they to whom it appears. Recently a correspondent in Ohio wrote me that he had beheld such a mysterious eye, and forthwith I wrote him for particulars, — after this book was nearly all set up in type. The subjoined reply came to hand, which I deem of so great importance to those who aspire to seership, that I have caused it to be printed herein. Says the writer : —

"T—— C——, Ohio, Jan. 9th, 1869.

"Now for the particulars of that eye, or whatever it was. For some time past I have been wearing a bandage (not the improved magnetic arrangement, but the first crude substitute therefor) — this bandage was of linen, with half-a-dozen thicknesses of heavy paper over my eyes and forehead at night, — and tried to see through them, according to the directions laid down in your book, 'Dealings with the Dead,' and your first monograph on clairvoyance. I began this practice immediately after purchasing a magnetic or magic mirror (a second-grade trinue). As I sit at the present time, I soon see a pale golden light, seemingly misty, frequently cut with flashes of electric or magnetic light. In this soft, pale, golden light, there appears a spot of deep-yellow gold moving about, sometimes in a circle. After watching it for some time, it resolves itself into something like an eye, with a dark, deep-blue pupil; then into a ring of gold around the eye-centre; then into a lighter ring of blue, resembling an eye. I first saw this object two or three weeks after I bought the mirror. The first object I saw at all was in the evening when sitting back toward the bright lamp-light. I had sat about twenty minutes, impatient and discouraged at seeing nothing but a black mirror, when suddenly the appearance described above showed itself near the left-hand lower corner of the disk, slowly passing upward two-thirds the way toward the right-hand upper corner, when it suddenly disappeared. This has been repeated several times, with variations. Its size was that of a silver dime. I thought it was a usual thing, hence paid but little attention to it; I am certainly not a seer, but thought I was tending that way. I was not satisfied, because I could not get a likeness when I wished to. I can get answers enough, but not always reliable, though the future may reveal something more satisfactory.

"Yours, etc.,

Now I know cases wherein that identical spot of golden light has resolved itself into an ethereal lane through which magnificent supernal realities have been seen; and other cases wherein full faces have grown out from it, and the perfect forms and features of the dead been fully beheld and recognized. More than that: I have known three persons, at the same time, in broad daylight, see the same things, — a magnificent living picture, embodying the most splendid and arabesque scenery; and I am satisfied that whoever can see even a single cloud pass across the mirror's face can, if they but pursue the matter, very soon develop their latent powers of clairvoyance or seership. But not all can do so, for I have known persons to try for quite a length of time without succeeding, owing to some organic difficulty born with them; persons who will probably never become clairvoyant while in the body. At this point I will state, that in any case of difficulty in developing the psycho-vision, the wearing of the magnetic bandage on the head at night, and the magnetic plate on the body by day, will go far toward removing the disturbance and obstructions, besides exerting a positive curative effect, if the party be at all ailing. . . .

Again, while reading the printer's proofs of this work, another letter, from a lady in Oswego, N. Y., reaches me, pertinent to the matter of the volume. I quote : —

"Oh, let me tell you that my dear father has gone home since I left Boston. . . . I was far, far away from him. . . . I was looking in my mirror, not even knowing he was ill. . . . I saw my father's face, his beautiful face; and it seemed as white as snow, and his reverend hair as white as his face. . . . Since that he has come to me just as I used to see him long, long years agone, in the splendid prime of perfect manhood. And he conveyed to me these blessed words, — '*My child, I am not dead!*'"

Reader, such a *proof* of immortality can be had by no other means, and is worth all the medium talk, and oblique, indirect, and far-fetched communications in the world, ten thousand times over.

Another proof, while I write. The Cambridge gentleman, alluded to
a while since, has just related to me the following strange experience with
his mirror : —

"A short time ago while looking in my mirror, my attention was ar-
rested by the appearance of an object resembling a vast and distant
mountain. Even while I gazed upon its craggy outlines, it changed into
the semblance of an enormous cloud, moving toward the top of the glass,
dividing itself into two parts, and gradually evanishing from sight. And
now a train of curious, but indistinct, objects began to pass in panoramic
order across the sublime field of the marvellous glass. Suddenly the
mirror became radiant with auroral light, and things flashed across it
with electric speed. Barren regions, utterly destitute of verdure; rug-
ged mountains, awful chasms, fearful precipices passed, — immediately
followed by a majestic sweep of planets, stars, suns, systems, galaxies,
in awful splendor and unutterable majesty. They sailed away, and
seemed to leave me solitary and alone, standing hard by the confines, as
it were, of an awful, vast eternity — a stranger in an unearthly clime —
an infinitesimal mote in space — the merest speck in existence — the
nearest approach to Nothing, without power to comprehend the vast,
boundless, limitless vault before, beneath, above, and around me.
Amazed at the awful sublimity of the scene, I was on the point of calling
for an explanation, which I undoubtedly should have obtained, when my
solitude was broken by the entrance of one of those cast-iron, matter-of-
fact men, whose only idea is the dollar; and to my great annoyance the
mirror ceased to reflect the image of the Eternal, and the séance for that
time was ended."

The superiority of Psycho-vision to the so-called mediumism of the
day, for all purposes whatever, is too apparent to need further argument.
Spiritual manifestations subserve the grand end of demonstrating the
sublime fact of post-mortem existence, but, as a revelative power, otherwise is of but very little use ; and the quality of mediumship unquestionably injurious, because it is impossible to *know* whether the possessing
invisible is good or evil. A "Hearsay" is good ; but "I see and know,"
is a great deal better. The thought here intended to be conveyed, was
very elegantly and forcibly expressed by Dr. Uriah Clark, a man who had
the bravery to openly denounce the imposture and pretence of modern
spiritualism, in defence of a truer and higher kind, direct from God.

" The trifling tricks passing for modern spiritual phenomena pale into
insignificance before the magnificent phenomena of Nature and the Revelations of God in human history. 'You brave o'erhanging firmament,'
'fretted with golden fire;' you cloud-capped mountains pushing their
white cones into the heavens; you glorious landscapes sweeping into the
distant horizon; the murmur of myriads of sentient existences swarming
the air and earth around; the eternal roar of old ocean, and the æolian
melody of the morning and the evening breeze; the songs of woodlands,

and the whistling of hurricanes; the waves and tides sweeping around our globe; the world, wheeling through empires of endless space, — the occult forces flashing in lightnings, and rolling in thunders vibrating the universe; the unseen currents coursing through every fibre of the wonderful mechanism of our being; these minds within us, anon making us feel like heroes, martyrs, gods facing fire, flood and fiercest battle; these hearts of our ours pulsating with hopes bounded only by eternity, — all these are revelations of Almighty God, and prophets of the soul's unending destiny."

A finer peroration, or a grander one, I never yet heard fall from human lips. Yet this is called defection, and treason against the truth. It may be so, but if it is, then set me down as loving all such defection, and glorying in just such treason. If there were more of it, this were a great deal better world. . . .

Enforced celibacy, continued singleness, is, in the vast majority of cases, an unmitigated curse, beside being an outrageous swindle on God, and fraud upon Nature; alike to be dreaded and shunned by all men, and especially by all women, who were never created or intended to

" Waste their sweetness on the desert air,"

by any manner of means, for which reason I fully justify any and every woman in getting a husband by any art or means within her power, — magic, magnetic, sympathetic, or, if she can do it, by the magnetic love-charms, — amulets, or the mysterious magnetic powders, — not of the modern tricksters, but of "La Petite Albert," which, however, the wise ones may laugh and sneer at, have, for one hundred and fifty years demonstrated their astonishing magnetic power in affectional directions. On my table lies a copy of that work, in old French, printed at Lyons in 1758, full of strange secrets on the points here mooted; and which book it would take a large sum to buy from me. I fully agree with that author, that any man or woman is fully justified in resorting to any crimeless means in order to retain or regain the love of wife, husband, or friend; hence my advice in this book, but more especially that contained in my works on "Love and its Hidden History," "The Master Passion; or, The Curtain Raised," and the forthcoming reprint of "The Grand Secret; or, Physical Love, its Mysteries Revealed," which I intend to incorporate in the two first-named books in future editions, this present year, 1870. Meanwhile, those who want special information can enclose a fee and write me for it.

It is disheartening, not to say disgusting, to read the nauseous advertisements in the papers of conscienceless wretches, who have "love powders" for sale, which have no more virtue than a piece of chalk. And yet the idea involved is based upon a truth as eternal as the universe, which truth is, that peculiar substances can be charged with the efflux or aura of the human being (witness the science of homœ-

opathy, to say nothing about haunted houses, etc., and the startling facts
of spiritual mediumship). The substances thus chargeable are few, rare,
and costly; yet such *do* exist, and (it takes two persons of opposite sex
to do it) they can not only be filled with the specific magnetism of a person, but can be filled with the aura of hadean lust and passion, just as
the Voudoos effect their incontestible magnetic spells; or they can be
charged with divinest love, and be impressed spiritually with a mission
to any soul with whose body they shall come in contact. It matters not
to me who denies this fact of the magnetic universe; *I know it*, for I have
seen a deserted wife bring to her feet her recreant lord; I have seen a
great actor re-win the love of his wife, whom another member of the same
opera troupe stole from him, and I have seen a betrayed and almost
ruined girl arrest the career of him who first betrayed, and then left her
out in the cheerless cold of an infernally hypocritical world. To save
people from being victimized by charlatans, it is as well to inform them
that in no case can anything be charged with the power by one person
alone; hence, money sent for such things is worse than thrown away.
Two persons, of opposite gender, *one of whom must be the party who desires to affect a third one*, must conjoin in the process of infiltrating, by
will, by hope, by the breath and finger-tips, the neutral substances with
the specific power and magnetic quality designed; nor can it be done in
any other way whatever, because there *can be no magnetic evolution unless
the magnetic law of minus and plus, positive and negative, magnetic and
electric, be observed.*

But what *are* the materials that can be charged with a specific human
magnetism? I reply, — The negroes of Africa and our own land know
of and use hundreds, — herbs and roots mainly; but science, in the hands
of the late Baron Van Riechenbach, whose researches into the mysteries
of light, heat, odics, chemism, and magnetics cannot be overvalued,
has thrown a flood of light on the subject, so that now we know what
substances are the best; and fine steel-filings, iron by hydrogen, sugar of
milk, chloride of gold and lactucarium, well manipulated together in
proper quantities and exact proportions, by two persons, in a glass mor-
tar, can be charged so powerfully as to exert a specific influence upon
even a dumb animal, much less a human being. Perhaps it is well that
such a preparation is very costly, requiring much time, trouble, and expense, else wrong uses might be made thereof. And, besides that, it is
absolutely essential that certain ingredients must be furnished from the
person of the individual who proposes to be benefited by its use; and
without this the thing is useless, because the specific magnetism will escape. It is to be sewed in the garment, or worn by the party to be
effected; not swallowed, or taken inwardly. Albeit there are substances that may be, to the same end. I do not propose to name the something else, unless I know to whom it is imparted. To rakes, seducers,

and libertines, *no!* to heart-sick, unloved wives, yes; and also to victims of the other gender. But to none others if I know it.

There are millions of "old maids" in America and Christian Europe, but I doubt if as many can be found in all Turkish Europe, India, China, Arabia, Japan, Syria, and the Islands of the Seas, as exist within the limits of New England alone! Why? Because the white woman, everywhere, is ignorant of the foundation-laws of love! the wonderful measures of magic (magnetic) forces underlying the master-passion of the human soul; while the white man, as a general thing, is altogether too surface in the matter; is not properly struck or impressed by the immense value and importance of children, nor of the principles which subtend the laws of their proper and normal generation. They are too much absorbed in dimes and dollars, political, and other perishable ambitions; too fond of place, power and *éclat;* their love for woman is tempestuous, sensual, intermittent, superficial, based on physical organization mainly, without either a mental or moral *élan* to give it soul and substance. They win easily but wear badly; to correct which evils, so far as possible, is why I write, and publish edition after edition of my works: "Love and its Hidden History," "The Rosicrucian's Story," "The Master Passion; or, The Curtain Raised," "After Death," "Ravalette,'' and others bearing upon the general subject, any, or all of which, if the lessons they convey be well observed, will smooth the surface of Marriage-land.

For the benefit of those who specially require cerebral or brain magnetization, I have made arrangements with an artisan here to furnish an invention admirably calculated to exert a specific and positive electromagnetic power on the brain, directly above the eyes, and right on the frontal region of the head. There can be not the slightest doubt that these plates will prove extremely useful in the direction indicated, and serve as an electric curative power as well, in catarrh, headache, neuralgia, sleeplessness, and general nervous unrest. The cost of these fine head magnets, as well as those alluded to elsewhere, will be FIVE DOLLARS. The head-plates should be bound over the eyes and forehead at night on retiring, and be worn there an hour or two, or all night long. The body magnetic plates may be worn over the breast, sides, back, abdomen, or limbs; and these especially are a curative agency for *all* forms of disease, especially such as originate in disordered nerves; not surpassed, if equalled, by any other in existence.

Before closing this work, I beg to again enforce upon those who would attain to a positive development of lucidity, the absolute necessity of perfect nervous quietude during the process; because every departure therefrom, every excess, physical, mental, emotional or sexual — every abnormalness, of whatever nature, are just so many and effective bars to its attainment. Everything may be done in moderation, but whoever goes beyond the mark, treads upon the "dead line" of Clairvoyance. Will is the primal Power. Love the central Force. Persistence is the Road.

To such as have faith in the things underlying outer sense, who realize that we are floating in a sea of mysteries, that the reality of all things lies deeply hidden behind a thick veil, which only the strong and patient soul can raise or penetrate; to those especially who have provided themselves during the last twelve years with good and perfect instrumentalties; and to those who have demonstrated their importance in the deeper researches of magnetic science and philosophy; and to such only, is this book and the subjoined code of rules for their use presented. And these rules are exact copies — rendered into English — of those in use by all oriental seers, with the exception of the extracts from De Novalis and the Masters, both of which I copy from my first work on internal vision, long since out of print.

I. To have impatience (in these things) will delay, or totally prevent, success. But unto the true seeking soul cometh ever the real light of the divine magnetic power of true magic. But it cometh in its fulness only to the spirit that is self-possessed and calm. Remember what the Grand Master, himself a genius rare, and, therefore, a true seer, says: "The true Rosicrucian, the acolyte, the adept, reaches forth for the infinite, in *Power* and *Goodness*, which are the keys that unlock the gates of glory; and he sees, hears, knows, and healeth the mental, physical, social, moral, and domestic ills of humankind, by means of his goodness and his mighty secret, whereof but few in an age are naturally possessed, and still fewer attain to, for want of WILL and PATIENCE. For only the children of the empyrean, by nature or adoption, are admitted to the treasure-house of the underlying, and overflowing real. Such, only, have the true medical and supernal inspiration, and inhale the diviner breath of God . . . Whosoever hath a strong will, and purity of purpose, may, if they elect, unbar the doors of mystery, enter her wide and strange domain, and revel in knowledge denied to baser souls."

De Novalis says: "The fortuitous is not unfathomable; it, too, hath a regularity of its own. He or she that hath a *right sense* for the fortuitous, hath already the signet and seal of a royal power, naturally to know and use, not all mystery, but much that lies very, *very* far beyond the ken of mortals who are not thus endowed by nature, or have not grown thereto by experience and choice. Such persons can readily determine *truly* that which to others less gifted, or with less COURAGE, WILL, PERSISTENCE, PATIENCE, and quietude, must forever remain unknown. For one with these qualities necessarily commands both information and obedience from the viewless intelligences and subordinate powers and agencies of the universe. Such can seek destiny for others, in her own halls; solve her riddles by her own laws; and read, as in an open book, the future, — the things that shall befall an inquirer in all that pertaineth to body, soul, health, affections, and possessions; and, still casting forward and upward the soul's keen glance, can discern the final result and summing up of being, and all by means of the phasoul and phantorama, as revealed to the Searcher's vision on the surface of the Symph, the magic mirror, the peerless disk of La Trinue."

II. There are glasses of three grades : the mule, or small, neuter ; the female and the male. The first is small, but fine ; more a philosophic toy than of practical use ; has two foci, is good for clouds and flame, symbols and shadows ; but the magnetic filament is very thin, and the two foci not always mathematically true ; they are quite easily warped and broken, cost but little, and are mainly used by fortune-telling, vagrant gypsies of the lowest class, and who are not able to procure a higher and better grade trinue.

The mirror next in size to the imperfect sort just described, is, in mirrorists' parlance, called well-sexed, or female, because its foci are true, its polish superb, its power great, and sensitiveness most remarkable. There are magic mirrors in existence really not much superior to these last, valued at fabulous sums. For instance, the one that covers the back of the Sultan's watch, for Abdul Aziz, of Turkey, possesses one of rare beauty, seeing that it consists of a single diamond concaved out ; and its value is something over $400,000. The late Maha-rajah Dhuleep Singh possessed three : one an immense diamond, the other an enormous ruby, and the third composed of the largest emerald known in the world ; and yet, despite the enormous pecuniary difference in value between these and a trinue of the second order, it is doubtful if the former, for special uses, can ever equal the latter. For a glass of that grade will hold a magnetic film nearly *eight inches* in thickness, flattened on the top, quite as good as a first grade male mirror for seeing all things, and only inferior thereto in not affording a magnetic surface sufficiently extended to admit of the finer and grander phantoramic displays ; and not thick enough to enable the seer to readily affect distant persons, or to fix the called-up images or simulacra of distant persons, or the locality of the absent living or dead. But, for all ordinary purposes, it serves admirably, and, in my judgment, is altogether superior to the celebrated crystal globe, belonging to Charles Trinius, of San Francisco, California, for which $3,000 was offered and refused. They are more expensive than the male-glass ; more of them are made and imported ; and they are the kind generally in use throughout the Western Continent.

Not long ago, a " Reform " paper publisher declared he had no faith in mirrors ; and yet, within a month thereafter, published column after column to prove the reality of precisely the same thing. For both the principles, rationale, methods and results, are *identical ;* namely, spiritual photography. But, in reality, the man only objected to the one, because it didn't originate among the faithful of his peculiar household, and commended another form of the same thing, because it *did* thus originate, and was backed up by wealthy lawyers, doctors, judges, and moneyed men, most of whom, judging from their style of argument, possessed more greenbacks than brains. I and my friends are poor, and can't afford to buy up the proprietors of papers, which, you see, makes all the difference in the world; and hence there is a marked contrast in regard to the claims of wealthy Tweedledee, and impecunious Tweedledum, who are, after all, precisely right, because exactly on the same ground. Spiritual and electric photography is, and ever was and will be, true; and crystal seership, and mirror visions, and such photography, are one and the same thing, operated by the same laws and principles, and underlaid and subtended by precisely the same wonderful esoteric chemistry; and the only difference, if any, lies in the fact that but few persons can get spiritual photographs, while a great many can obtain very satisfactory, but evanescent, pictures, by means of a differently sensitized plate,— a fact I have seen demonstrated hundreds of times, as thousands of others have whom I never saw, heard, or knew.

The male mirror is superior to either of the others. Its foci are *four inches apart*. The basin is over *seven inches* by *five in the clear ovoid*, and of course its *field* is immense. They are better adapted to *professional use* than private experiment, because they are capable of, and frequently do, exhibit *three* separate and distinct vivoramas, at one and the same time, to as many distinct on-lookers. I have often wished I could make these mirrors; but that is impossible, as three continents furnish the materials composing them. And even the frames and glasses must be imported from beyond the seas; as must also the strangely sensitive material wherewith the sympathetic rings are filled; concerning which rings and their brightening, when the future is well, and their strange darkening, when evil impends, or friends fall off, and lovers betray, the quadroons of Louisiana, as well as the women of Syria, could tell strangely thrilling tales. And in consequence of the importance attached to these rings and mirrors, counterfeits of them have been, in times past, put forward, albeit the parties who obtained them were themselves to blame, seeing that but one person — Vilmara — ever imported either to this country.

III. No mirror or ring must be allowed to be handled much, if at all, by other than the owner thereof; because such handling mixes the magnetisms and destroys their sensitiveness. Others may *look* into them, holding by the box in which the frame is kept, but *never* touching either frame or glass.

IV. When the glass surface becomes soiled or dusty, it may be cleaned with fine soap-suds, rinsed well, washed with alcohol, or rubbed with a little fluoric acid, and then polished with soft velvet or chamois leather.

V. A mirror must not be neglected; but should frequently be magnetized by passes with the *right* hand, five minutes at a time. This is calculated to keep it *alive*, and give it *strength* and *power*.

VI. Passes with the *left* hand add to its magnetic *sensitiveness*.

VII. The longer time, and frequency of its use, the better it becomes.

VIII. The somnifying or magnetizing power of the glass is obtained to a greater degree than is possible by hand-mesmerism, by looking at its centre in perfect quietude. It will magnetize many who defy mesmerism.

IX. When used, the mirror's back must always be *toward* the light; but its face *never*. *That* is fatal to its visional power.

X. The position of the glass, held or placed, must be *oblique;* that is to say, its top must lean *from* the on-looker.

XI. When amateurs, or several, look in at one time, it should be suspended; but must then be touched by nobody at all.

XII. The proof of the proper focus or position of the glass is when no image or thing whatever is reflected in it. Change its inclination, or move the head, till a *clear, plain*, whitish-black, deep-watery *volume* is seen, which will not be till the magnetism has time to collect. That surface is the magnetic plane of the mirror; and in and upon it all things seeable in a trinue are beheld.

XIII. The first thing seen are clouds. They appear to be *on* or in the mirror, but in reality are not so, but on the upper surface of the magnetic field above it. That magnetic plane collects there from the eyes of the onlooker. Persons of a magnetic temperament, — brunette, dark-eyed, brown-skinned, and with dark hair, — charge it *quicker*, but no more *effectually* than those of the opposite temperament, — blonde or *blondette*, — who are electric in temperament.

XIV. The male is not so *easily* developed into seership as the female sex; but become exceedingly powerful and correct when they are so. Virgins see best; next to them are widows.

XV. In all cases the boy before puberty, and the girl in her pucilage, make the quickest and sharpest seers. Their magnetism is pure, unmixed, unsexed; and purity means power in all things magnetic and occult.

XVI. White clouds are favorable; affirmative; good.

XVII. Black clouds are the exact reverse: inauspicious; bad.

XVIII. Violet, green, blue, presage coming joy, — are excellent.

XIX. Red, crimson, orange, yellow, mean danger, trouble, sickness, "beware," deceptions, losses, betrayal, slander, grief, and indicate surprises of a disagreeable character.

XX. To affect a distant person, invoke the image. Hold it by will, and fix the mind and purpose steadily upon the *person;* and whoever he or she may be, — no matter where they are, — the telegraph of soul will find them, somewhere within the spaces. But, observe this law: Nothing is surer than, if the seer's purpose be evil, it will react upon him or herself with terrible effect, sooner or later; wherefore all are strictly cautioned to *be* and *do* good, only; for : —

XXI. Remember the aerial spaces are thronged with innumerable intelligences, celestial and the reverse. The latter have Force; the former possess Power. To reach the good ones, the heart must correspond. In many ways will they respond, when invoked with prayerful feelings; and they will protect and shield from the bad, — and there are countless hosts

of the bad on the serried confines of the two great worlds, — Matter and
Spirit : myriads of grades of them, whereof the *puling*, phenomenal spirit-
ualist never yet has even dreamed.   These malign forces are many and
terrible ; but they can never reach or successfully assault the soul that
relies on God in perfect faith, and which invokes the Good, the Beautiful,
and the True.

XXII. The face of the mirror should *never* be exposed to the chemical
and actinic influence of direct sunlight, because it ruins the magnetic sus-
ceptibility, just as it does the sensitized plate of the photographer ; and no
mirror once spoiled can be made good as before, without sending it to
Europe to be re-made entirely.   Moonlight, on the contrary, benefits
them.   The back must not be tampered with, or removed, for any light
striking it will at once completely ruin all its magnetic properties ; hence
its careful sealing.   So also are extremes of heat and cold injurious to
them, because either will destroy the parabolic-ovoid shape of the glass,
which done, it is thenceforth useless, for it will no longer retain its hold
upon the magnetic effluvium from the eyes, — the sensitive sheet upon
which its clouds and other marvels are mirrored ; but it will roll off like
water from hot iron, and, in the words of Vilmara, " be good never — no
more ! "

XXIII. Whatever appears upon the left hand of the mirror-looker, as he
gazes into it, is real ; that is to say, is a picture of an actual thing.

XXIV. Whatever appears upon the right hand, as he looks into it, is
symbolical.

XXV. Ascending clouds or indistinct shadows are affirmative replies to
questions that may be asked, — if silently, it makes no difference.

XXVI. Descending clouds are the negations to all such questions.

XXVII. Clouds or shadows moving toward the seer's right hand are
signals from spiritual beings, indicative of their presence and interest.

XXVIII. When they move toward the left hand of the seer, it means,
" Done for this time," — the séance is ended for the present.

To conclude : I neither import, manufacture, have made, or keep these
mirrors and rings, for sale.   The small ones are of but little value ; the
next size it is almost impossible to procure, although occasionally one can
be obtained.   The large, professional, but more expensive and immense-
ly better ones, are much easier to get hold of, but must be handled very
tenderly.   When I want either mirrors or rings, for myself or a friend, I
either go to head-quarters and select them personally, or procure the
services of an expert.   *The members of the Fraternité de la Rosecroix*, are
hereby informed that they must procure these things also, at head-quarters,
as I have no time to spend for those who know the *true points of the com-
pass ;* and all *such must travel straight towards the setting sun*, and at the *end
of the journey the* LIGHT *will be seen !* I write this, because desirous to
avoid unnecessary correspondence, being fairly deluged with letters on
the subject, very few of which contain a clerk's fee, or even return pos-

tage stamps, a tax I propose to avoid henceforth. People also write me if I receive pupils in the mystic sciences; and if I still teach the art of forecasting the future by Plato's Numbers and the Oriental Pfal? The answer is, Yes, *when paid for it; not without.* And the fee for replies to the meaning of any series of seven numbers, simple or compound, chosen at random from any figures from 1 to 408, is fifty cents *each reply.* But if there be seven numbers sent, chosen from between the figures 1 to and above 408, up to 1000, the fee for replies to any seven such numbers is seventy-five cents. If chosen from between 1001 and 2000, the fee is one dollar. If from between 2001 and 3010, the replies often occupy whole sheets of paper, and the fee is two dollars and fifty cents upward. The numbers 1 to 408 are simple; from 408 to 1000 double; from 1000 to 2000 compound; from 2001 to 3010 involute numbers, all bearing strange, weird meanings, warnings, or prophecies, concealed beneath the underlying soul number. But I am no longer able or willing to do these things, or to teach the art without a *quid pro quo,* — rent-paying, bread-buying, future-providing pay.

At this point I expressly wish to caution people not to spend either their time or money in the pursuit of occult science, either through mesmerism, magnetism, or the mirror method, unless such persons have a natural bias, tendency, qualities of mind, or general aptitude thereto; for, if they do, disappointments may head them at every step of the journey. On the contrary, I consider the power of positive seership of such immense value and importance, that no expense of time, patience, and means is too great in order to obtain it. I have known persons who spent much time and money in the effort to reach interior vision without the slightest success, because there was some primal, organizational obstacle in the way. Some have failed, and given it up entirely; but after a time the sight came, as it were, without effort, which was so because their repeated efforts had given them an impetus in the proper direction; and in the fulness of time the power was duly born. I have also known numerous cases wherein the power of seership resulted from the very first trial, and thereafter continued to intensify and deepen, until their hearts had but little more to long for in that specific direction. To all, I say, If you think you have the latent quality, by all means seek to strengthen and develop it. But if not, then save yourself unnecessary waste of time and trouble.

P. B. R., Boston, Mass., P. O. Box 3352.

LOVE!

ITS HIDDEN HISTORY!!

THE BOOK OF THE CENTURY!

MOST REMARKABLE BOOK ON HUMAN LOVE

Ever Issued from the American Press. Two Vols. in One.

A BOOK FOR

*WOMEN, YOUNG AND OLD; FOR THE LOVING; THE MARRIED,
SINGLE, UNLOVED, HEART-REFT PINING ONES;*

ESPECIALLY FOR

UNHAPPY WIVES, AND LOVE-STARVED ONES OF THE WORLD.

DIRECT, EXPLICIT, AND VALUABLE COUNSEL

CONCERNING THE

GREAT CHEMICO-MAGNETIC LAWS OF LOVE.

THE MASTER PASSION;

OR, THE CURTAIN RAISED.

WOMAN, LOVE, AND MARRIAGE; FEMALE BEAUTY, AND POWER;
THEIR ATTAINMENT, CULTURE, AND RETENTION.

Warren Chase on "Free Love" — Origin of Uterine Diseases — Terrible power of a
Woman's hate — Love *vs.* Passion — The stormy life — The love-cure — The love-curse —
Mothers in-law — Strange power of woman's love — Once-in-a-whilish love — A hint for
husbands — True marriage — Gusty love — The tides of love — A hint for unloved wives
— How to regain a lost affection — The law of fixedness in love matters — The magnetic
attack — When woman's love has most conquering power — A secret revealed — An extraordinary thing concerning parentage! — Relative love power of brunettes and blondes
— Men don't know how to make love — *The how !* — Man's periodicity of love — Woman's — The difference — Sex and passion after we are dead — Singular — The Cypri-

"LOVE" AND THE "MASTER PASSION."

an's prayer — Love well and marry early — Beauty and Art — The chemistry of love and beauty — How to increase love-power — Aspasia, Diana de Poictiers and the bath of beauty — Peter of Lombardy, the Rosicrucian, and the elixir of life — *What it was — Ninon D'L'Enclos*, young at ninety years, and how she did it — Strange secret of *life-prolonging!* — Vilmara and his mysterious cordial — Curious method of Madame Tallien for preserving her youth and beauty — The whole art of adornment — Skin, hair, eyes, teeth — Protozone — This section alone is worth the price of ten such books to every female in the land, be she old or young ; for it contains the whole secret of magnetic female beauty — The magnetic plate for nervous ladies — Turkish Harems — how they beautify themselves — Toilette articles — How to make and use them — Bad effects of two in one bed—Fun as a doctor—Difference between the sexes—Rather curious—The Roman daughter—Touching story—A latter-day sermon—The social evil—Extraordinary means resorted to by the higher grades of "loose women" to preserve their beauty, and restore it when lost—Protoplasm, and how to increase it—Huxley's theory —Scandal—Running upstairs, and the heart disease — Freeman B. Dowd, Luke Burke, Charles Swinburne — Peerless trio—Boyd of Minneapolis on true marriage—Divorce, is it a real remedy for an unhappy marriage? — The Woman's Grand Secret — Beecher on "The secret sins of youth " — The chemical origin of "sin" — Portrait of the Girl of the Period, and the girl of the future — Marriage in 1970 — A startling scientific fact concerning human blood — What becomes of harlots after death ? — Tests of the love nature by the color of the eyes — Very singular, and true — A certain cure for dyspepsia, page 100, second part — Whom not to marry — A philosophic caution to those who love — The essence of marriage is consent — What the Rosicrucians are — The rights of a lover and husband are the same — A lover's and brother's not so — The true rule of divorce — Legislators, take notes of this — Heart, not mind, carries sex along with it — Marriage not dependent on a ceremony — A fashionable woman's prayer — Prayer of the Girl of the Period— Why some people marry—A Hottentot's picture of heaven—To PHYSICIANS ESPECIALLY — An entirely new theory of nervous diseases, and methods of cure — Prompt, certain, and complete — Trouble in the love nature the cause of untold sickness — Means of cure — The use and abuse of amatory passion — Change of nervous centres — Frightful consequences thereof — Discovery of the philosopher's stone ! — Magnetic exhaustion, and the remedy — Voodoo John, of New Orleans, who completely subjugated woman — Magnetic fascination — Vampires — Life leeches — Consumers of souls — A thrilling warning — The whole terrible mystery of Voodooism revealed — The cause and cure of all evil — Want of true love — The death of love and its life — Valuable hints to medical men — A new theory of cure and a faultless one — The celebrated " Leg-Love " Secret of Gautier — Dickens' trouble with his wife — Why wives generally ruin their talented husbands—A hint to women — A very curious paper on incest — *Proving a man's brother to be nearer of kin to him than is his father or mother* — Byron's alleged incest — Singular cause of wedded misery and discontent — Its certain cure — The *only* cure for the deadly personal sin — Why wives hate their husbands — General Grant Wilson on marriages among men of genius — A splendid paper, by a splendid man — Socrates, Xantippe, Aspasia, Diotima, Domenichino, Milton, Alecto, Salmasius, Bacon, Coke, Shakespeare, Montaigne, Moliere, La Fontaine, Rousseau, Beaumarchais, Whitlocke, Saville, John Wesley, Dryden, Steele, Coleridge, Sterne, Churchill, Byron, Shelley, Bulwer and his wife, Fuseli, Hobbes, Locke, Bentham, Spinosa, Kant, Gibbon, Barrow, Chillingworth, Hammond, Poe, and other genii — Why unhappy benedicts are celibates — Carlyle and his wife — How the Scotch giant lives at home — The underlying law of human genius — A hint to mothers — Freeman B. Dowd — Grand master of the Rosicrucians — Reference to seership, and the seven magnetic laws of love, whereby the unloved gain it, and lost loves are firmly rebuilded — A strange and mighty power — How to retain a husband's love—Old-maidhood-and how to avoid it—The how! [The work called " Seership," containing the Oriental Woman's Art of Love, and *direct* statement and *application* of the seven magnetic laws of love, was put to press after the above volumes were written. Its price is *three dollars, and can be had only direct from this office.*]

Of the large double volume, octavo work on Love and the Master Passion, the universal testimony is that no *other. book* in any language is so full, plain, clear, explicit, and exhaustive. Its price is $2.50, and 30 cents postage — direct from my office *only.*

I have just completed my work on Seership, and will forward a synopsis of contents upon application by letter, which must contain two stamps.

P. B. RANDOLPH, Boston, Mass.

NERVO-VITAL REMEDIAL WORKS,

BOSTON, MASS.

WE respectfully announce, that, with improved facilities, and larger capital, .we are now producing a *very superior* grade of PROTOZONIC and PROTOPLASMIC remedies, and at greatly reduced prices, and of a finer quality than is possible by any other medico-chemical house in the country; besides which, we own the sole rights of the processes on the continent.

These remedials are the only ones that will cure the effects of solitary vice in either sex; — brain-softening, loss of semen, incipient insanity, deficient vitality, inpotence, sterility, and all troubles originating in nervous exhaustion. They are made solely by. Dr. P. B. Randolph, their discoverer, and are sold only by this house, and its authorized and certificated agents. Special prescriptions will be made for any given case, either from diagnosis and description, or analysis of urine by ourselves or others, as certain cases require different combinations of the organic and medicinal elements constituting the bases of the series.

The improved Nervo-Vital remedies will hereafter be sold at the following (considering the enormous cost of their production) exceedingly low scale of prices: CONCENTRATED PROTOZONE, absolutely pure, the most perfect nervous invigorant in the world, for physicians' and druggists' use, in pound flasks, $5 each; PHOSODYN, pure, a splendid remedy for all forms of nervous disease, exhaustion, debility, brain trouble, mental wandering, and unequalled in complaints peculiar to females and persons of sedentary habits, in pound flasks, $5.00.

Double concentrated NEURINE, pure, a magnificent chemical triumph; a perfect agent for the cure of DYSPEPSIA, and blood troubles, and the purest tonic invigorant stomachic cordial, in flasks, $5.00 each. BAROSMYN, an excellent agent, and unequalled for all cases of kidney and bladder difficulties, the diosma crenata being skilfully combined with phymylle, glycerine, and PROTOZONE; in pound flasks, $5.00.

We also prepare an ALEXIPHARMIC REMEDY, believed to be a perfect antidote to all poison in the blood, from a simple rheum to the most inveterate scrofula, putrid, ulcerous and syphilitic taint in the blood, bones or any organ, no matter of how long standing, or what its type. Such forms of disease cannot exist where these remedials are faithfully used; price $5.00. CHLORYLLE, for the use of consumptives and delicate anæmic cases; per flask $5,00. We also prepare a fine RHEUMATIC Remedy, superior to any yet evolved by medico-chemical research; price in pound flasks, $5.00.

We prepare a special, and very powerful, yet harmless remedy,— only when ordered, which is a specific for Diabetes, Bright's Disease of the Kidneys, Leucorrhœa, Gleet, from excess, Strains, Kidney and Bladder, Catarrh, Ulcerations, and other causes, unexcelled by any article ever manufactured, and as yet without an equal; price $5.00 and $7.00. None of these celebrated agents are in any sense "Patent Medicines," but a series of well-tested medical agents, believed to be superior to all others in existence for their peculiar specialities.

The majority of cases require a course of from two to four of these remedials, and we discount twenty per cent. under such circumstances. Dealers and right-holders are allowed a discount in proportion to the amounts ordered at one time. Remittances must be made by P. O. orders, or Registry.

We are prepared to supply all orders, and to give territorial rights for the exclusive sale and use of these preparations, and to give special instructions to those who desire to make nervous diseases in all their forms a speciality; said instructions embracing an entirely new system of gynæcology, enabling the practitioner to treat female complaints, and obstinate renal and brain diseases, with a power and success never attained before the discovery and use of the above series of Nervo-Vital remedials.

RANDOLPH & Co., *Special Chemists.*

Laboratory and Office, Boston, Mass.

AFTER DEATH:

THE

DISEMBODIMENT OF MAN.

The Publishers are happy to announce a new edition of this masterly work, — the most thrilling and exhaustive book on the subject ever printed.

REVISED, CORRECTED AND ENLARGED.

Price, $2; Postage free.

BOSTON:
RANDOLPH · AND COMPANY.

CONTENTS.

CHAPTER I.

•

CHAPTER II.

CHAPTER III.

CHAPTER IV.

•

CHAPTER V.

CHAPTER VI.

CHAPTER VII. •

CHAPTER VIII.

CHAPTER IX.

CHAPTER X.

CHAPTER XI.

CHAPTER XII.

CHAPTER XIII.

CHAPTER XIV.

CHAPTER XV.

CHAPTER XVI.

CHAPTER XVII.

APPENDIX.

Also just published, a new edition of the

PREDICTION CHART, or SYMPH.

PRICE $1; POSTAGE FREE.

This extraordinary production is based on the Oriental idea of the "PFAL." Certain it is that no oracle ever yet produced, so marvellously indicates the occurrence of events yet unacted on the theatre of personal life as this, and withal it is so simple that a child can comprehend it in an instant. Close the eyes, ask a question or leave the event to answer itself; raise the finger and let it fall upon the Chart. The answers and the prophecies will astonish you, and the direct agency of the loved and gone before, be clearly recognized. It must be used to be known.